THE KEY TO DIVINE TREASURES

By

EMMANUEL ABRAHAMS

Order this book online at www.trafford.com
or email orders@trafford.com

Most Trafford titles are also available at major online book retailers.

Printed in the United States of America.

ISBN: 978-1-4269-5811-3 (sc)
ISBN: 978-1-4269-5812-0 (hc)
ISBN: 978-1-4269-5813-7 (e)

Library of Congress Control Number: 2011902950

Trafford rev. 02/22/2011

 www.trafford.com

North America & international
toll-free: 1 888 232 4444 (USA & Canada)
phone: 250 383 6864 ♦ fax: 812 355 4082

INTRODUCTION

For every treasure of God, there is a key and the key is the anointing. If the LORD does not anoint you, you cannot enter into those privileges. In this book I am going to bring to you the lessons I have learnt over the years about the anointing - how to receive it, so that you can enter into the treasures of God. The anointing is a secret of God, which is only available to those that are close to Him. As we study this fascinating subject, I am sure you will discover how to get all the things that God has reserved for you and also learn to increase your potential to greater things in the Kingdom of God. The greater the anointing of God on you, the greater your accomplishment in this Kingdom will be. 'For to everyone who has, more will be given, and he will have abundance; but from him who does not have, even what he has will be taken away. (Matt 25: 29)

CHAPTER 1
WHAT IS THE ANOINTING

"The Spirit of the Lord GOD is upon Me, because the LORD has anointed Me to preach good tidings to the poor; He has sent Me to heal the brokenhearted, to proclaim liberty to the captives, and the opening of the prison to those who are bound; to proclaim the acceptable year of the LORD, and the day of vengeance of our God; to comfort all who mourn, to console those who mourn in Zion, to give them beauty for ashes, the oil of joy for mourning, the garment of praise for the spirit of heaviness; that they may be called trees of righteousness, the planting of the LORD, that He may be glorified" (Isa. 61:1-3).

The Spirit of the Lord was upon the Anointed One because he was anointed. The only reason the Spirit did not go somewhere, or come around him, but was upon him was because he was anointed by God. The Spirit of God and the treasures of God do not come to anybody but those anointed by God - not those anointed by men. If you are not anointed, the Spirit of God cannot come upon you. "Therefore, I have said to you that no one can come to Me unless it has been granted to him by My Father" (John 6:65).

In my walk with the Lord, I have learnt that God is very selective. In the days of Abraham, He did not chose the entire family of Abraham to reveal himself to – He chose only Abraham. In the time of Enoch, God chose to walk only with Enoch not all the people that called on the name of the Lord. He did same with Noah. Another thing I have learnt about

God is that He loves to delegate responsibilities and duties to others. That is why He uses people to touch the lives of others. He delegated the care of the earth to man. When He wanted to save the Israelites, He sent Moses. When He wanted to save the world He sent his son Jesus. These are the basic principles behind the anointing. God chooses an individual and delegates work to him or her, He then backs him up by releasing His Spirit, power and every resource he will need to accomplish that assignment for Him. The mark of choice is the anointing.

To be anointed is to be chosen and assigned by God to a duty or a work for Him - "...that He may be glorified". It is because of this reason that the Lord will give His power and grace to His anointed because he becomes the direct representative of God. It so happens that whoever is dealing with the anointed one is dealing with God, whoever touches him touches God. A clear illustration of this is the way our public institutions work, for example a policeman on duty is a representative of the state, so when you deal with him you are dealing with the state. If you attack him, you attack the state and you are punished.

Every child of God is called to be the light of the world but most do not become because they lack the anointing. This is clearly explained in the letter apostle Paul wrote to Timothy – "But in a great house there are not only vessels of gold and silver, but also of wood and clay, some for honor and some for dishonor. Therefore if anyone cleanses himself from the latter, he will be a vessel for honor, sanctified and useful for the Master, prepared for every good work" (2 Tim. 2:20-21). So anyone can be anointed by God and be useful in a specific area of life for the Lord but you must first qualify for the anointing to receive the total backing of God in that area. That is the purpose of this book, to help you to receive and understand God's anointing for you.

WHAT IS THE ANOINTING?

The anointing is a special package that God gives you because you are anointed by Him. It is the divine supply needed to do the work assigned you and this includes power. To be anointed means to be chosen by God. "For many are called but few are chosen" (Matt 20:16). Many claim to be called by God but few are chosen by Him. To be chosen by Him, you have to go through training and development to be anointed by God. Some people are chosen before they were born, some became chosen after they have proved themselves through training and development. When the Spirit of God comes upon you, it will give you a sign which is definite and specific to each individual. What I feel or the sign I receive when the Spirit comes upon me is different from what sign you will have but there will be a sign. That is what men of God say that they "sense" the anointing. You need the anointing of God, which is God's package to function in the work. This is what we also call the unction.

SYMBOLS OF THE ANOINTING

We most often symbolize the anointing with the oil. In fact it is common to interpret the term "to anoint" as to pour oil. It comes from ancient customs. It was very common in Israel to pour libation with oil or wine, but the most common was oil. Oil was used to mark places and stones, so once oil is poured upon an individual or stone, the individual or stone is marked out. Jacob marked Bethel with oil, Samuel also marked kings out with oil. "Then Jacob rose early in the morning, and took the stone that he had put at his head, set it up as a pillar, and poured oil on top of it. And he called the name of that place Bethel; but the name of that city had been Luz previously" (Gen 28:18-19).

Then Samuel took a flask of oil and poured it on his head, and kissed him and said: "Is it not because the LORD has anointed you commander over His inheritance?" (1Sam 10:1).

So he sent and brought him in. Now he was ruddy, with bright eyes, and good-looking. And the LORD said, "Arise, anoint him; for this is the one!" Then Samuel took the horn of oil and anointed him in the midst of his brothers; and the Spirit of the LORD came upon David from that day forward. So Samuel arose and went to Ramah (1 Sam 16:12-13).

The purpose of anointing with oil was to physically mark out what God had already chosen. The oil symbolically represented the presence of God's power. The level of God's oil in your life represented your level of consecration in the eyes of God.
The anointing is the total package that God gives to the anointed to do or accomplish what he has been anointed to do.

I must emphasize that there are two kinds of anointed people:
- Those who are anointed before they were conceived and
- Those who have to work to prove their qualification for the anointing.

I do not know why God made it so but it is as if He made some main staff and others auxiliary staff. He gives the standby staff the anointing after He is sure that you can handle and use the anointing. Once I was praying about it and the Lord told me that there are those He has created and sent into the ministry but at times there are some people He did not call but as they desire and work hard for God, He calls and anoints them. For those ordained before they are conceived, the Lord waits until the appointed time then He calls them to service. Their previous lifestyle may or may not tally with the present call. This is how God calls, cleanses and ordains people whose lifestyles appear unacceptable. Every servant of God knows for certain when God called him. When you answer the call, God sets you apart, cleanses, trains and anoints you. It is then that you can receive the anointing. So many things work together for the anointing to come upon a person. We will study these things in course of this book.

Jeremiah was an example a person ordained by God for a purpose before he was born - "Before I formed you in the womb I knew you; before you were born I sanctified you; I ordained you a prophet to the nations" (Jer 1:5).

The anointing gives you signal when God is ready to work or tells you what to say or do in a given situation.

Moses and Joshua are examples of men called but with different timing. The ministry of Joshua depended upon the fulfillment of the ministry of Moses. Joshua was to be only seen and highlighted through the ministry of Moses. Some ministries birth other ministries. Another example is Elijah and Elisha. Elisha continued the work of Elijah so if Elijah did not do his work we will not see Elisha. Gehazi, a servant of Elisha, through greed disqualified himself from the call so he could not be anointed (2 Kings 5:20-27).

Those chosen before the foundation of the world are pacesetters in their area of assignment. You may be the next giant for God. The choice is God's;

you can only make your call sure. "Therefore, brethren, be even more diligent to make your call and election sure, for if you do these things you will never stumble; for so an entrance will be supplied to you abundantly into the everlasting Kingdom of our Lord and Savior Jesus Christ" (2 Peter 1:10-11).

We will look at the separate components that work together to make the anointing sure and effective.

God anoints individuals for different purposes. If God calls you to heal the sick, He gives you anointing - that is, the total package of different things needed to heal the sick. It may be the spirit to discern demons, sweet words of encouragement that can give someone the strength to overcome the illness, power to cast out demons so that the demons causing certain sickness will be cast out, etc. The package of the anointing is total and effective for the task ahead of the anointed. No two anointing are the same, they can be similar but not the same, each anointing is unique. We cannot even compare the anointing of a master and his student as seen in Elijah and Elisha. God in his own prerogative adds and removes to adjust an anointing to the next person's personality.

COMPONENTS OF THE ANOINTING

There are many components of the anointing, but I will give you the basic components. Even ministry gifts are part of the Gifts that make the component of the anointing Eph 4:7-11

But to each one of us grace was given according to the measure of Christ's gift. 8 Therefore He says:

"When He ascended on high,
He led captivity captive,
And gave gifts to men."

9(Now this, "He ascended" — what does it mean but that He also first descended into the lower parts of the earth? 10 He who descended is also the One who ascended far above all the heavens, that He might fill all things.)

11 And He Himself gave some to be apostles, some prophets, some evangelists, and some pastors and teachers
NKJV

Spiritual gifts

Spiritual gifts are the fundamental building blocks of the anointing, the gifts are used for the ministry as the apostle Paul wrote concerning spiritual gifts - "But the manifestation of the Spirit is given to each one for the profit of all" (1 Cor 12:7). It is these spiritual gifts that you use to touch lives , but as you use them they grow and get better and God increases the gifts you have or add new gifts to the ones you have. I will also like to state that there are more spiritual gifts than the ones written in 1 Cor. 12:8-11. Gifts like visions, dreams and many others were not recorded. But the truth ultimately remains that the spiritual gifts are given by God to serve his purpose through the individual. " but one and the same Spirit works all the these things, distributing to each one as he wills" (1 Cor12:11).

Holy Spirit

You cannot be anointed without the Holy Spirit coming upon you. When you receive the anointing the Holy Spirit comes upon you, Jesus told his disciples "… for John truly baptized with water, but you shall be baptized with the Holy Spirit not many days from now" (Acts 1:5). In the prophesy of Isaiah, we quote "The Spirit of the Lord GOD is upon Me, Because the LORD has anointed Me To preach good tidings to the poor; He has sent Me to heal the brokenhearted, To proclaim liberty to the captives, And the opening of the prison to those who are bound; (Isa 61:1). Concerning king David we read "Then Samuel took the horn of oil and anointed him in the midst of his brothers; and the Spirit of the LORD came upon David from that day forward (1 Sam 16:13). Concerning King Saul we read in 1 Sam 10:6 "Then the Spirit of the LORD will come upon you, and you will prophesy with them and be turned into another man." This means that, when you are anointed, the Spirit of the Lord must come upon you to transform you into another man – another man enabled to do the work the Lord has given you. That is why when a man of God is ministering, you see a different person from the one you know. Just as Jesus said in John 3:3, "Most assuredly, I say to you, unless one is born again, he cannot see the Kingdom of God." Flesh and blood do not operate the power of God but the transformed individual. That is why Jesus told the disciples "But you shall receive power when the Holy Spirit has come upon you; and you shall be witnesses to Me in Jerusalem, and in all Judea and Samaria, and to the end of the earth" (Acts 1:8).

Power

You cannot be anointed without power. Even Jesus, our Anointed One, was anointed with power for His ministry - "...how God anointed Jesus of Nazareth with the Holy Spirit and with power, who went about doing good and healing all who were oppressed by the devil, for God was with Him" (Acts 10:38). Power is important for the work of the Lord, without God's power, the work cannot be done. It takes divine power to produce divine results and it takes God's power to do God's work. The work will not be accepted in the eyes of God without his power in it. That makes power vital.

Fire

On the day of Pentecost, the anointing came down with fire. In Acts 2:3, we read, "Then there appeared to them divided tongues, as of fire, and one sat upon each of them. The anointing must and will always come with fire as John the Baptist said in Matt 3:11-12 "He will baptize you with the Holy Spirit and fire. His winnowing fan is in His hand, and He will thoroughly clean out His threshing floor, and gather His wheat into the barn; but He will burn up the chaff with unquenchable fire". God releases fire with his anointing for two reasons:

a.   To purify the life of the man of God and his environment, and to make sure no demons can work to manipulate or pervert the gifts of God. The fire is unquenchable fire to ensure continuous purifying and purging. We must be continuously purified to be fit for the work.

b.   For the quickening and revival of gifts. That is why till today we believe in revival fire.

Dove of God

Doves have always been special messengers of God's power and declaration. In Genesis, Noah sent a dove and it returned with the message of an olive leaf, he sent it again after seven days and the dove did not return to prove that the time was right for him to leave the ark (Gen 8:8-12). When God wanted to anoint Jesus He sent a dove with the declaration of that message and power. "and John bore witness, saying, I saw the Spirit descending from heaven like a dove, and he remained upon Him" John1:32 "when he had been baptized Jesus came up immediately from the water; and behold, the heavens were opened to Him, and he saw the Spirit of God descending like a dove and alighted upon Him. And suddenly a voice came from heaven, saying this is my beloved son in whom I am well pleased" (Matt. 3:16-17). A messenger without a message is not a messenger. God's dove is the carrier of the message of God to your life. It tells you what He is actually doing in the work and in your life. "For what man knows the things of a man except the spirit of the man which is in him? Even so no one knows the things of God except the Spirit of God. Now we have received, not the spirit of the world, but the Spirit who is from God, that we might know the things that have been freely given to us by God. (1 Cor. 2:11-12). This is the reason apostle John taught that " but the anointing which you have received from Him abides in you and you do not need that anyone teach you but as the same anointing teaches you concerning all things, and is true, and is not a lie, and just as it has taught you, you will abide in Him" (1John2:27). If you learn, listen and obey the guidance of the anointing and learn well you will know what to do in all situations and the anointing will also flow. Because it gives guidance on what to do to get the anointing always working. And it stirs you to use the anointing to produce results.there have been many times I have seen doves come upon people and they have prophesied.

Grace

The Bible said that" and with great power the apostles gave witness to the resurrection of the Lord Jesus. And great grace was upon them all" (Acts 4:33). The Bible equated great power with great grace because they are all components of the anointing. Grace is not only unmerited favor but it is also spiritual strength. It is the backbone of a man of God; it enables him to withstand every attack of the enemy and to deal with the enemy. "Finally, my brethren, be strong in the Lord and in the power of his might. ....." (Eph. 6:10). Grace is what enables you to resist the devil that he flees. It is what enables you to go through the challenges of the ministry. It is what enables you to survive every onslaught of the devil. An example of grace at work is found in Acts 9:19-22 when Apostle Paul became convinced that the people could not believe, but instead of being discouraged, he was stronger. That inner zeal which stands out in contrary situations for a man of God to still forge forward despite all odds is what we call grace and it comes with the anointing.

Oil

Oil is what causes the anointing to shine, it polishes the gifts and makes the gifts to function and grow. If the flow of oil stops, the anointing will die because it is the oil that keeps the fire burning. "And he said to me; what do you see? So I said I am looking and there was a lamp stand of solid gold with a bowl on the top of it, and on the stand seven lamps with seven pipes to the seven lamps. Two olive trees are by it, one at the right of the bowl and the other at its left." (Zech. 4:2-3). " Then I answered and said to him, "What are these two olive trees — at the right of the lampstand and at its left?" And I further answered and said to him, "What are these two olive branches that drip into the receptacles of the two gold pipes from which the golden oil drains?" Then he answered me and said, "Do you not know what these are?" And I said, "No, my lord." So he said,"These are the two anointed ones, who stand beside the Lord of the whole earth." (Zech. 4: 11-14). The anointing is a signal that the labourer has just received the needed tools for work to start. The servant of God has received the enabling power to do the work. Oil is what makes you have impact just as the oil keeps the fire in the lamp burning and oil get the moving parts of an engine working. Oil is used as a preservative; it is what sustains the impact of your prayer and ministry it gives you the strength to keep on moving in the work of God. There was a time in my ministry that the prayers we prayed were not making impact and prophecies were not coming to pass and preaching was not producing fruits. I sought the face of God on it and he revealed it to me that the oil in the ministry was being drained away so there was no impact. It was after the drainage was blocked that I saw changes and improvement in the ministry. You therefore have to be careful and guard it well for it will make or break you. The anointing is all you need to be on top of your spiritual life and work in the house of God.

CHAPTER 2

HOW TO RECEIVE THE ANOINTING

In Matt 22:14 we read, "For many are called, but few are chosen". This statement by Jesus is a profound one. So many people parade around that they are called by God to do ministry. Some know that they are called but because of the challenges involved in doing the ministry, they do not want to answer the call to the ministry. God gives the anointing to do the work, which makes the work easy. Many are laboring and suffering in the ministry because they have not received the anointing that comes with the call. Such situations make ministry difficult.

When God calls you, you are ushered into a period of preparation and testing, God gives you the grace to survive until the appointed time. When you prove yourself through the testing then God chooses and anoints you as a confirmation.

"But as we have been approved by God to be entrusted with the gospel, even so we speak, not as pleasing men, but God who tests our hearts" (1 Thess 2:4). Apostle Paul knew that you could excel in the work of God only when God trusts you, and that trust is a result of your proven heart after the trials.

Jesus said in Mark 9:49 "For everyone will be seasoned with fire, and every sacrifice will be seasoned with salt". If every sacrifice will be salted before

God accepts it, then God must also season you with fire before He can take your body as a living sacrifice.

Your heart

The motivation of your heart is crucial and critical for God to trust you with His anointing. "The heart is deceitful above all things, and desperately wicked; who can know it? I, the LORD, search the heart, I test the mind, even to give every man according to his ways, according to the fruit of his doings." (Jer 17:9-10). Before God will anoint you or bless you, he will look at the heart behind what you do and he will reward you for the good heart you have. Therefore, if your heart is not correct, He will not bless you. "For where your treasure is there your heart will be also" Luke 12:34 - if you treasure God's work even during the trial period your heart will be there and God who sees your heart he will bless you. God calls so many people, but the motivation you have for God's work is the yardstick for His blessings. You receive what you bargain for; if you choose to build a church and take the material benefits when the church grows, that will be your bargain and no more, but when you decide to set up a church, work at it and wait for God's blessing, that will be your bargain and that is what you will receive. "Nobody can receive anything except it is given to him from above," if you do not have the anointing, you do not have it. No matter what you do, you do not have it. It is only God who gives it, it is not quoting scripture or positive confession but only God. So if you have been relying on scripture quotation to think that you have the anointing check it again because it is only God who gives you the anointing when he can trust you with it. God will trust you only when he has tested you through trials. Trials come for two main purposes; to test your values and to expose your weakness. Some will claim that afflictions are not from God true but he permits it for His purpose. "And we know that all things work together for good to those who love God, to those who are the called according to His purpose." (Rom 8:28) You will discover that it is because of the call of God on you that you go through those afflictions.

I personally believe that the apostles in their epistles shared their wealth of experience and maturity. They were not just expounding new Christian ethics and laws but shared the deep things they had personally learnt from the walk with the Lord, received through revelation, and practiced which had worked for them. It was not just a law on Christianity that they ordered but they shared what they had practiced and learnt that worked to the believers and also the revelations they had personally received of God and the understanding they had acquired in their walk with God is what they taught. "Moreover I will be careful to ensure that you always have a reminder of these things after my decease. For we did not follow cunningly devised fables when we made known to you the power and coming of our Lord Jesus Christ, but were eyewitnesses of His majesty." (2 Pet. 1:15-16) "That which was from the beginning, which we have heard, which we have seen with our eyes, which we have looked upon, and our hands have handled, concerning the Word of life — the life was manifested, and we have seen, and bear witness, and declare to you that eternal life which was with the Father and was manifested to us — that which we have seen and heard we declare to you, that you also may have fellowship with us; and truly our fellowship is with the Father and with His Son Jesus Christ." (1 John 1:1-2). Therefore, it was out of their practical experience that they shared their teachings because they had seen it at work and known how it worked. From this, we can deduce that they were telling us what would happen and helping us to understand and to know what to do when it happened. Concerning your heart with God they had a lot to say. "My brethren, count it all joy when you fall into various trials, knowing that the testing of your faith produces patience. But let patience have its perfect work, that you may be perfect and complete, lacking nothing." (James 1:1-2). Having a perfect heart is God's ultimate for you, until then you will go through trials that will eventually lift you from one level to another. The level of heart in the eyes of God depends on how far you allow trials to transform you.

Faithfulness

Another quality God will look for before He gives you great anointing is faithfulness. Anointing is inclusive of God's power over creation that He delegates to you to use in the affairs of men on His behalf. God looks at your faithfulness to Him; he looks at your attitude and seriousness in obeying His instructions and the usefulness you attach to things that concern Him. And how you put to use or if you do make anything useful out of what the Lord has given you. He looks at you to see if you are a good steward of anything in your care, before he will give you a tangible anointing. Jesus told his disciples that "he that is faithful in little things shall be ruler over much," and of Moses, God said, "… He is faithful in all My house." (Num 12:7). God can give you his power only when he knows that he can trust you with it, if you will use it effectively and profitably and will not abuse it. God must be sure that when He gives you work, you will stick to it whether it is convenient or not.

Loyalty

Loyalty is a critical disposition for the move of God in your life. If you are not loyal then God will also switch off his backing on your life. There is an anointing that God puts upon you as a backing for your ministry. If you are not loyal, God will not bring down that backing power. That anointing that God sends upon you is what you use to reach people and perform miracles. That external anointing is what announces you because it quickens what is inside you and releases it. "for the eyes of the Lord run to and fro throughout the whole earth, to show himself strong on behalf of those whose heart is loyal to Him,..." (2 Chron. 16:9). If your heart is not loyal to the Lord and to your fellowman, God is not going to release a great anointing, because the anointing also comes with the responsibility of being a delegate of God, and a custodian of God's power. If men cannot be depended upon you, then God cannot depend on you - "Lord, who may abide in our tabernacle? Who may dwell in your holy hill? He who walks uprightly, and works righteousness, and speaks the truth in his heart; he who does not backbite with his tongue, nor does evil to his neighbor nor does he take up a reproach against his friend" (Ps. 15:1- 3), in Ps. 24:3-5, we read, "Who may ascend into the hill of the LORD? Or who may stand in His holy place? He who has clean hands and a pure heart, who has not lifted up his soul to an idol, nor sworn deceitfully. He shall receive blessing from the LORD, and righteousness from the God of his salvation."

The Lord once told me that many people come to Him for selfish reasons. Most people have idols in their heart when they come to God and idols in their dealings with their fellowman and that is why God is not blessing them. Most people associate with people not with a sense fellowship in mind but with the intention of making money out of them. You can make money genuinely from a friend, but if there is no transparency in your dealings with your fellowman, then you have an idol in your heart.

Many men of God are doing the work of God with the sole motivation of living a flamboyant or superfluous life. I am not condemning luxury, but when it is the sole motivation for the work then your heart is lifted up to an idol. Are you motivated in your dealings with your fellowman by loyalty or by selfish ambitions? If you become loyal to God, he will bless you beyond your wildest dreams and imagination. If you are motivated by the benefits of the work then you will not achieve much because God will not back you with more anointing or he will not release it at will - "but seek ye first the Kingdom of God and his righteousness and all these things shall be added to you" (Matt. 6:33). So in everything you do be sure your allegiance is first to God and then to your fellowman – "You shall love the LORD your God with all your heart, with all your soul, and with all your mind.' This is the first and great commandment. And the second is like it: 'You shall love your neighbor as yourself.' On these two commandments hang all the Law and the Prophets." (Matt 22:37-40).

After the apostles in the book of Acts dedicated themselves to seek the Lord in prayer and to minister the Words of life to the people, the hand of the Lord upon them became greater. Jesus was always motivated with seeking the lost and healing the sick and God was with Him. Apostle Paul also became great because of his motivation for the Kingdom and his relationship with God, "for I determined not to know anything among you except Jesus Christ and Him crucified" (1 Cor. 2:2), "… in mighty signs and wonders, by the power of the Spirit of God, so that from Jerusalem and round about to Illyricum I have fully preached the gospel of Christ. And so I have made it my aim to preach the gospel, not where Christ was named, lest I should build on another man's foundation," (Rom. 15:19-20). Therefore, the Apostle Paul was willing to go as far as possible to spread the gospel that is why God did signs and wonders with him. If you are not a loyal person, you cannot receive the anointing of God. If you cannot stand by your pastor in good times and bad times, what makes you sure, you will stand by the God of that man of God - your pastor. That is why many of the Israelites died in the wilderness because they could not walk with the God of the Moses whom they did not respect and stand by. Since you cannot stand by a man of God when he is in trouble, the God of that man of God will not give you his power because you cannot be trusted. Why? You may ask. The reason is that anointing brings trouble; it actually invites the devil to attack you because the anointing is a precious commodity spiritually. The bigger the anointing, the bigger the troubles. As a man of God, the most painful thing is to have nobody to stand by you, encourage and strengthen you in times of troubles and mistakes.

At times, the Lord will send you to work, and it will bring trouble; you will not always receive a pat on the back for doing the work of the Lord, sometimes it brings disgrace, reproach, threats and other things you did not bargain for. Elijah ran away from Jezebel's threat because he was discouraged; he thought his work did not bring any change, so God gave him Elisha as a companion and an encourager. Elisha, who stood by Elijah, went on to be so anointed of God that even when he died his bones could still raise the dead. The path of an anointed man of God is a lonely one and when you stand by such men, God appreciates it a lot, and rewards you. Until you master the process, he cannot give you certain positions of responsibility. promote you. What you have not experienced you cannot handle. If you have not learnt how the path looks like God cannot trust you with the responsibility of carrying his power and the warfare that goes with it. Some people are loyal when it is convenient or when they understand and agree with what is going on. Such people should forget of great power because the power of God and the workings of God cannot be understood at all times. What could Hosea the prophet do when the Lord told him to marry a harlot? Today, we would have quoted 1 Cor 6:15-16 to prove the servant of God wrong and thereby hindering the work of God. If you are willing to go very far in the anointing then you will have to take unpopular decisions in obedience to the Lord. This obedience proves how loyal you are to God. You may not know or understand why you are doing it; all you know is that you are obeying your Master. I once preached a message I titled "What Do You Do If God Fails You," in this message I explained that it happens to anointed people at times especially when He is training you, He deliberately fails you for some time to prove you so that He can stand by you. Will you continue to believe in God and serve him even when he is not answering your prayers and the devil is giving you a beating? However, there is a level where He does not fail you because He has tried you and seen that you are worth standing by, as He told Abraham at Mount Moriah in Genesis 22. Ask yourself why will God heal some in a crusade and others are not healed? All I will say is what Jesus said "and blessed is he who is not offended because of me" (Matt 11:6). The anointing is a costly business, your credibility can be damaged, your integrity questioned but you still need to be loyal to God. Learn this lesson well because the devil will do anything to get you away from the anointing of God. Loyalty, come what may, must be demonstrated because the God of the man of God will reward you. An example is the life of David after taking Bathsheba and killing Uriah the Hittite, God punished David but everyone who left David in the time of crisis lost in the end. Ahitophel hanged himself, Absalom lost his life, and all the others suffered. No matter the faults of an anointed man stand by him. God will deal with him for his mistakes but you will lose most if you turn against him because the foundation of God with him is sure to always win all odds.

I used to ask why bad things happen to men of God or why men of God make certain mistakes and I discovered that God permits it to happen to prove to everyone that they are just human beings subject to like passions but they carry the power of the most High God. If you look at the life of men that were greatly used of God, with the exception of a very few each had a reproach on them. Apostle Peter denied Jesus three times, apostle Paul persecuted the church, king David stole another's wife, Abraham slept with his wife's servant Hagar, and Samson was a lover of foreign women. These are examples so that we do not repeat them as we also work at ourselves to be better. In case you fall into one, do not stay there get out quickly because these mistakes do not go unpunished especially with the devil hanging around looking for opportunity to destroy you. So do not dance with sin, it could burn you badly. King Saul lost his kingdom, King David had an upheaval, a coup, Samson lost his eyes, and his pride so there will always be consequences but God expects loyalty and values loyal servants.

Service

An anointed man is a servant of God, if you do not know how to serve, you cannot carry the anointing, because the anointing is given to serve mankind not to lord over them, we already have one Lord, the most High God over all men "… the manifestation of the Spirit is given to each one for the profit of all" (1 Cor 12:7). Some people received powerful anointing because of the men of God they served, for instance, Joshua received anointing because of Moses, Elisha received anointing because of his service to Elijah, if he did not serve he would never have received a double portion, Samuel received his anointing because of his service in the house of God. If you do not find anything to do in the house of God or for God then you are not ready to be anointed. Elijah received his anointing because he wanted to turn the heart of Israel back to God. Service is an important condition for receiving the anointing. Are you willing to do any kind of work no matter how low for the sake of God? Will you sweep a church floor, dust chairs, scrub washrooms, usher, or sing if need be, or will you say it is not your level, so you will not do it? How low you are willing to stoop for God, will determine how much God will back you. Isaiah was willing to serve and God and God made him one of the greatest prophets. Furthermore, God does not like lazy people; everyone God called was busy going about their business when God called them to serve him. If you do not serve, then God will not anoint you, if you are willing to serve the Lord, he will anoint you"…the hand of the Lord shall be known to his servants and his indignation to his enemies" (Isa 66:14b).

Reverence

To be anointed, you must value people, you must have deep reverence for God and his servants. What you do not value or respect, you cannot have or benefit from. Just as it happened to the officer on whom the king leaned when Elisha prophesied of abundance. "So an officer on whose hand the king leaned answered the man of God and said, "Look if the Lord would make windows of heaven, could this thing be? And he said, in fact, you shall see it with your eyes, but you shall not eat of it" (2 Kings 7:2). God will anoint those who fear and respect him and those he has anointed "… He permitted no one to do them wrong; Yes, He rebuked kings for their sakes, saying, "Do not touch My anointed ones, and do My prophets no harm" (Ps.105:14-15). God also anoints those who are under authority. If you are under the authority of a person, if you reverence the fellow because of his authority he has above you, God will also promote you to that position because you respect it. You must appreciate God's creation and see value in people; you must endeavor to help them out of their problems.

Voice of God

The voice of God is not easily identified; it is recognized over time of growth. Jesus said my sheep hear my voice and obey. What you must recognize is that the sheep started as a lamb and grew to a sheep. Recognizing the voice of God will take a process of discovery because God speaks in diverse ways and the way He speaks to me will be different from the way He speaks to you. "God who at various times and in *various ways* spoke in time past to the fathers by the prophets" (Heb1:1). As you grow to recognize the voice, it will develop in clarity until it comes to the point of no ambiguity. It takes time to get to that stage, just as the sheep grow to recognize the voice of their Master so will you have to grow and work at it to recognize the voice of God if you desire.

To recognize the voice of God, you need to master who is speaking. Knowing the other counterfeit voices is a plus.

1. You must know that there are many voices that speak to you, so you must find out the spirits behind those voices - that is discernment, "Beloved, do not believe every spirit, but test the spirits, whether they are of God;

because many false prophets have gone out into the world. (1 John 4:1). It is the spirit behind the voice that a man of God listens to that makes him a false prophet. To guard against this, try the spirits and be sure if it is of God. This is also what leads to false doctrine and teaching you must be careful about the Spirit behind the thoughts you get and the voices you hear.

2. You must recognize the ways God speaks to you. Just as heb1:1 says God has many ways he speaks so you must be quick to recognize Himwhen he speaks. This is very critical if you want to operate tin the anointing. Because God releases power to do his works so you need to hear God and obey so that the power of God will accomplish what it came down for.

Biblical principles

A lot of time people claim that you must judge prophesy with the word of God i.e. the scriptures, and if it does not conform with the scriptures than they are false. If God tells you to wave and his Spirit will heal people, will you say that because it is not written in scriptures you will not do it and deny people who were to be healed their healing. The Bible is full of stories of men and woman who set precedents for others to follow. If the God we serve does not change, then don't you believe that God can use you to set a new precedent? In judging prophesy and the things of God, the Bible lays certain foundation down which we must obey. First Jesus said that his words are a rock upon which you can build your life. "Therefore whoever hears these sayings of mine and does them, I will liken him to a wise man who built his home on a rock" Matt. 7:24. Apostle Paul explained it further that it is a foundation for what we do in our life. But we have a responsibility to build from there 'for no foundation can anyone lay than that which is laid, which is Jesus Christ. Now if anyone builds on this foundation with gold, silver, precious stones, wood, hay, straw, each one 's work will become clear; for the day will declare it because it will be revealed by fire; and the fire will test each one's work, of what sort it is" (1 Cor 3:11-13), which means that what you build on the foundation is important and the Bible says " unless the Lord builds the house, they labor in vain who build it" (Ps 127:1)

If the scripture is true then it is important to hear the voice of God in our days. The reason that people make noise about testing prophesy with scripture is because they are so Spiritually lazy that they cannot know what is of the Spirit of God and which is of the devil. So anytime they get an idea, check and can support from the Bible then it is of God. they forget the devil quoted scriptures to try to deceive Jesus but the Spirit of God then quickened other scriptures in Jesus to counter the devil. The Bible did not say that we should judge scriptures but rather the Spirit behind what is being taught or said must be judged to find out if it is of God. In fact, the devil will rather use the scripture to his advantage than go out of scripture so beware. It is not all the scripturally sound teaching that is from God but anything that is from God will be scripturally sound. What God will not teach you are his secrets which he shares with his close confidants for their use only . when you know God and his voice well then he can take you beyond the foundation of scriptures to another level in God to build a house for him. The Pharisee felt the teachings of Jesus were not scriptural but they did not know that He was the son of God. To be under authority is to listen to and obey the voice of God when he speaks. This will let his authority to be released always because God knows you reverence him - "therefore, since we are receiving a Kingdom which cannot be shaken, let us have grace, by which we may serve God acceptably with reverence and godly fear" (Heb 12:28).

Fellowship

Fellowship with God and Christians is very important to receive the anointing. Jesus said that when two of three are gathered, he is in their midst. The God of the quiet is also the God of the crowd. You do not have to be alone; you have to be with a group for there is strength in numbers. Heb 10:25 buttresses this - "not forsaking the assembling of ourselves together, as is the manner of some, but exhorting one another, and so much the more as you see the day approaching." God is a God of order so he wants to create a platform for you to receive and learn from Him as he builds you to be anointed. He expects you to be among believers so that your life can be enriched. Also, your fellowship with God is important "Jesus answered and said to him, "If anyone loves Me, he will keep My word; and My Father will love him, and **We** will come to him and make **Our** home with him" (John14:23). God loves to fellowship, if you spend time to fellowship with Him, He will be so close to you and He will bless you beyond your wildest dreams.

The sovereignty of God

In closing this chapter, I want to make it clear that these above named attributes will not totally guarantee your reception of anointing because the ways of God are beyond understanding. God is sovereign and he does what He likes all the time. While we try to do our best, the ultimate decision lies with God. When we do these things, we (put ourselves in good standing for the anointing) <u>improve ourselves to be anointed</u> but the anointing will come from God at his own time - "Therefore, brethren, be even more diligent to make your call and election sure, for if you do these things you will **never** stumble; for so an **entrance** will be supplied to you abundantly into the everlasting kingdom of our Lord and Savior Jesus Christ" (2 Peter 1:10-11). I have seen people God anoints without following the system. Elijah did not serve under anyone. Abraham did not fellowship with people to receive his encounter with God. God anointed David before the above qualities were tested. Some people will pray and God will give them anointing, some will fast and pray before God will give them the anointing and for some God do will not mind them it is just as the scripture say "the lot is cast in the lap, but its every decision is from the Lord" (Prov 16:33). Therefore, do your best and leave the rest to God but when you do these things your chance is great and most of the time it will happen for you.

CHAPTER 3

GROWING IN THE ANOINTING

Everything that the Lord creates has life, which makes it living. Because it is living, it grows or it can die. In the same way, the anointing is a living force. It has to be nurtured and protected to make it grow and mature. It is always dependant on a conducive environment of the things of God, so it has to be sustained at all times in the presence of God. Jesus used a simple analogy. We read in John 15:1-2 "I am the true vine, and My Father is the vinedresser. Every branch in Me that does not bear fruit He takes away; and every branch that bears fruit He prunes, that it may bear more fruit". John 15:4-5 read "Abide in Me, and I in you. As the branch cannot bear fruit of itself, unless it abides in the vine, neither can you, unless you abide in Me. I am the vine, you are the branches. He who abides in Me, and I in him, bears much fruit, for without Me you can do nothing". All the things of God must be sustained in a God loving environment, if you are not connected with God, the anointing cannot be sustained and it will die. As you grow in using the anointing the anointing will grow. As the branch grows bigger and stronger, it can carry a bigger amount of sap which is the anointing, because it can make effective use of what it has.

God will never release to you what you cannot carry and make use of "…..for unto whoever much is given, of him shall much be required: and to whom men have committed much, of him they will ask the more"luke12:48b. And because you can do more, the anointing that is released is more, that is why the bigger the crowd the bigger the anointing that flows. But to come to that level of big crowd anointing you have to grow into it and growing is not an easy thing. In this chapter, I will give you the clues that you need to know about growing in the anointing. "And you cannot put new wine into old wineskin" (Mk 2:21-22), there must be a new person to carry the new wine or anointing, if you do not change into a new person you cannot receive the fullness of the new anointing. For the anointing to grow there must be a change, space must be created for more to be added. Your capacity must be enlarged to receive the increased anointing.

The presence of God

You need to be in the presence of God to grow in the anointing. Just as a fish out of water will die and a plant in a wrong environment will die. More so when the anointing is not in the presence of God or in the right environment it will die. So the lack of the presence of God and the lack of a conducive atmosphere for the anointing, will prevent the anointing from making impact. And the right atmosphere for the anointing firstly is the desire.

Desire

If you do not desire to be in the presence of God, the presence of God will not come near you. The presence of God can only come because you desire to experience God. Encountering God brings his presence down, God never goes to places he is not welcome. "draw nigh to God, and he will draw nigh to you" (James 4:8), if you desire to be with Lord so much that he is like the very air you breath, then his presence will walk in. "the Lord is with you, while you be with him: and if ye seek him, he will be found of you; but if ye forsake him, he will forsake you" 2 Chron 15:2. As you desire and seek for God very hard, he will walk into your life and the anointing will grow because he will cause it to grow since he is the source of the anointing. "Now He who establishes us with you in Christ and has anointed us is God, who also has sealed us and given us the Spirit in our hearts as a guarantee" (2 Cor 1:21). If you learn to live in the presence of God and abide in the presence, your anointing will grow. Living in the anointing and Spirit or presence of God is not an easy thing. Our human nature is not designed to live in the divine presence so it will not be easy but gradually you will adopt and by strange means, which is only known to God, you will be transformed to carry that glorious presence. That is why the face of Moses shined Ex. 34:28-30 and the face of Stephen shined as he beheld the Lord Acts 6:15 and Jesus also shined at the mount of transfiguration (Mk 9:2-4).

Prayer

Your prayer life also helps your anointing to grow, as you spend time before the Lord in prayer, the anointing is poured into your life because you go before the presence of God. an example is in the garden of Gethsemane "and there appeared an angel unto him from heaven, strengthening him" (Luke 22:43). It does not necessarily mean that you must pray for anointing but so long as you spend time before the Lord in prayer he will pour his Spirit in your life and nobody encounters the Lord and leaves empty handed. So be prayerful. As you spend more and more time praying, you will establish or rather build up a way or channel for the things of God to walk into your life. So the more you pray, you prepare the way for the Lord." In Isa 40:3-5, we read "The voice of one crying in the wilderness: "Prepare the way of the LORD; Make straight in the desert a highway for our God. Every valley shall be exalted and every mountain and hill brought low; The crooked places shall be made straight and the rough places smooth; The glory of the LORD shall be revealed, And all flesh shall see it together; For the mouth of the LORD has spoken".

The only way to prepare the highway for the things of God to flow in you life is prayer, as you pray, you break through Satanic hindrances and any other obstacles that hinder the free flow of the glory of God in your life. As you go before the Lord in diverse kinds of prayers, the obstacles, and structures that demons have planted in your life are destroyed. As you pray with all seriousness concerning various issues in your life, the demonic barriers in your life are brought down, and demons that stand in the way are destroyed and as angels come to you with answers. Demons that contend for your blessings are destroyed or defeated so the way is made clear for the Lord's glory to come down gradually. In addition, as you spend time in prayer, everything about you that stands in the way of God's glory is changed so you become a better person and spiritually stronger and you gradually understand the spiritual terrain and know how to walk it and be effective spiritually.

But I also want to sound a note of caution here; I have met a lot of prayer warriors who have not made any personal spiritual progress especially lasting progress. As I sought for answers, I discovered that most of them have confidence that they can pray their way through to get things, so the Lord is not glorified but rather their ability. So the Lord who should be glorified and remove the faulty foundations in their life also stayed away. Remember that what you ask in prayer, you receive it not because you are holy and righteous but because of the finished work of Christ, but the devil will look for faults in you life to steal or deny you your answers . That is why the apostle said in 2 Cor 3:5 "Not that we are sufficient of ourselves to think of anything as being from ourselves, but our sufficiency is from God". The privilege of asking and receiving from God should not be used as an excuse to overlook the real blessing of that privilege. This is for God to sanctify your life by drawing your attention to things that are wrong in your life for Him to deal with them, so that he can bring you close to Him and accomplish something tangible through you.

Fellowship
If you will grow, make progress or impact or improve, it always starts with a realization of a truth or a fact in your life or acquiring an understanding of issues deeper than you already had. This becomes the basis of which you can dissect a problem, see solutions to them or find practical and effective ways of using the anointing. And this transformation of outlook and mind comes only by the rubbing of minds and knowledge - "As iron sharpens iron, So a man sharpens the countenance of his friend" (Prov 27:17). Just as rubbing with a human mind (knowledge) can improve your mind, so can rubbing your mind with the mind of God improve yours - "… and be renewed by the Spirit of your mind" Eph. 4:23 which means let the outlook of your mind change. "and be not conformed to this world: but be transformed by the renewing of your mind that ye may prove what is that good, and acceptable, and perfect, will of God" Rom. 12:2 so as you develop fellowship with the Lord, he will open your mind to contain his mind. then you can do the things he wants to do through you, as a result of which you grow. "now we have received, not a Spirit of the world, but the Spirit which is of God; that we might know the things that are freely given us of God. which things also we speak, not in the words which man's wisdom teaches, but which the holy ghost teaches comparing Spiritual things with Spiritual. But the natural man receives not the of the Spirit of God: for they are foolishness unto him: neither can he know them, because they are Spiritually discerned. But he that is Spiritual judgeth all things yet he himself is judged of no man. For who hath known the mind of the Lord that he may instruct him? But we have the mind of Christ" (1 Cor. 2:12-16).

As we fellowship with God, you will begin to understand how the things of God work and he reveals them to you, as he rubs his mind with yours in times of fellowship. You will grow in the anointing because the knowledge of God will walk into you and you will change into a divine instrument of God. Revelation makes a lot of difference in your progress in life so if you do not catch revelations and understand the things of God, you cannot make impact with the anointing as expected of you by God. "but the people that do know their God shall be strong and do exploit" Dan. 11:32 knowing the full impact of such revelation in became the prayer of Paul for his disciples. "that the God of our Lord Jesus Christ, the father of glory, may give unto you the Spirit of wisdom and revelation in the know ledge of him: the eyes of your understanding being enlightened; that ye may know what is the hope of his calling, and what the riches of the glory of his inheritance in the saints, and what is the exceeding greatness of his power to us-ward who believe, according to the working of his mighty power" Eph. 1:17-19. which means that as you spend time communing with the Lord, he opens your understanding of things concerning you. As you also spend time with the Lord, you develop effective ways of communicating with the Lord and hearing from the Lord, which are critical to your success in the use of the anointing. Because you must know what God wants to do at a particular moment of ministration especially in critical cases that is brought to you or, the person will go back empty handed as he or she came to you. Maybe there is a hidden issue to be dealt with by God before the solution, but since you did not hear, it was overlooked and so the problem is not solved. So spending time in fellowship with the Lord is important for you to grow in the anointing.

Obedience

The key to God speaking and fellowshipping more with you is obedience. When you do not obey what he says, He will not speak to you or rather He may chose to punish you. Therefore, you must obey. You must be careful which voice you obey because the devil also speaks, so you must be sure it is from the Lord. The most serious mistakes I made in my early years of ministry were as a result of listening to voices that were not from God. At the time I started ministry I did not get any proper mentor so I learnt my lessons the hard way that is why I am writing this book to help those who will take the journey into the anointing. Once the devil gets you to make a mistake, he will make it difficult for you to get out or correct it so you have to be resolute to make right the wrong. That is why Apostle

Paul advised, "… having faith and a good conscience, which some having rejected, concerning the faith have suffered shipwreck …" (1Tim 1:19). You need to have a good knowledge of who is saying what for you to obey totally. Once you are sure of whom, you will obey even if you do not know his intentions. You can only obey him when you know and are assured of his voice. Jesus said, "Most assuredly, I say to you, he who does not enter the sheepfold by the door, but climbs up some other way, the same is a thief and a robber. But he who enters by the door is the shepherd of the sheep. To him the doorkeeper opens, and the sheep hear his voice; and he calls his own sheep by name and leads them out. And when he brings out his own sheep, he goes before them; and the sheep follow him, for they know his voice. Yet they will by no means follow a stranger, but will flee from him, for they do not know the voice of strangers." (John 10:1-5), "But you do not believe, because you are not of My sheep, as I said to you. My sheep hear My voice, and I know them, and they follow Me." (John10:26-27).

This statement of Jesus is the whole basis of obedience. You obey because you believe, you believe because you hear and know his voice and you know his voice because you have a relationship with Him. You can never have a true relationship with someone except you have known him well. You must gradually grow in obedience before you can obey Him in big things, if you do not mature in obedience, God cannot use you for great accomplishments. When it comes to obedience, the most important thing is to learn to recognize the voice of God. Some people claim that the scriptures is the voice of God, in as much as I agree that God gives us glimpses of His mind in scripture, let us not forget that the devil also knows scripture and he can use scripture to deceive you as he tried to do to Jesus. It is not every kind of scripture that should be applicable to some aspects of your life or you should depend on because Judas Iscariot obeyed scriptures by his actions, in fact, what he did fulfilled scripture{ Ps 69:25; 109:8} but he ended up with a bad name. (Acts1:16-20) so we must be careful which part of scripture you take. There is no scripture without spiritual and physical consequences – the consequences could be either good or bad. There also is this concept of the word, which is the scripture God is quickening in your life now - "it is the Spirit that quickens, the flesh profits nothing the words that I speak unto you, they are Spirit, and they are life" (John 6:63). It is taught that the Spirit of God will quicken a passage of scripture in your Spirit - this is the "rhema". It is a safe way if you master the process but personally, I believe in hearing the voice of

God and knowing the voice of God. That is a foolproof method but you can make mistakes in the growing process until you master the voice of God. You need the Lord to explain the scriptures He has written and make them all come alive to you because if you take the concept of "rhema" the Lord will use the Bible only as a reference book but the Bible should be a living document which flows in your life and is lived everyday. That is why Apostle Paul wrote, "You are our epistle written in our hearts, known and read by all men; clearly you are an epistle of Christ, ministered by us, written not with ink but by the Spirit of the living God, not on tablets of stone but on tablets of flesh, that is, of the heart" (2 Cor. 3:2-3). That is why the earlier Christians were more powerful than those of us today. Because they let the life of God flow out through them and in the process, their lives and words became the scriptures and the reference material for today. I always ask myself a question, why should we also not encounter the tangible glory of God and also be the living epistles? It is taught that if you have a problem, just look for scriptures concerning it and confess those scriptures and it will change you. I know it works because it is based on the principle of generating the faith to step out and handle it, and as you persist, the spirits at work may give way. Better still, I believe in another way, discuss it with your God, make Him a part of your burdens and He will help you to solve it and at the same time help you to grow in Him. However, concerning the voice of God I want to sound a note of caution, there is also the spirit of the antichrist that portrays itself as of God and will deceive you, so you have to be careful. That is why Apostle John wrote, "Little children, it is the last hour; and as you have heard that the Antichrist is coming, even now many antichrists have come, by which we know that it is the last hour. They went out from us, but they were not of us; for if they had been of us, they would have continued with us; but they went out that they might be made manifest, that none of them were of us" (1 John 2:18-19). This means that there are many deceiving spirits that come in different forms into the Christian's life and they deceive you to think that they are from Christ when, in fact, they are not. If the Christian is not careful, he will be genuinely deceived to think that he is on the right path. You must be careful because not all voices come from God. It is not every "stirring in your spirit" that is from God. In addition, Apostle Paul wrote "Now the purpose of the commandment is love from a pure heart, from a good conscience, and from sincere faith, from which some, having strayed, have turned aside to idle talk, desiring to be teachers of the law, understanding neither what they say nor the things which they affirm"

(1Tim. 1:5-6). Paul again warned Timothy on the arsenals of a good warfare: "having faith and a good conscience, which some having rejected, concerning the faith have suffered shipwreck," (1 Tim.1:19). Therefore, I always warn people to always check, to be sure, and to use commonsense most of the time. However, there are times when the Lord would speak and direct you to take steps that go beyond commonsense, in such cases you must have a deeper knowledge and conviction that it is of the Lord. In this, the Apostle John gives us advice - "But you have an anointing from the Holy One, and you know all things" (1 John 2:20). This implies that the Spirit of God gives you an inner knowing. What you need is to be full of the Spirit of God always, so that when something is not right you will know, and if it is from the Lord, you will know. There are certain times in one's walk with God that nothing seems to make sense but the only thing that keeps one going is knowing that the Lord is with you. Till the time you see the end of the tunnel.

Let me give you some clues about hearing the voice of God. God speaks in an audible voice but it is rare. Most people will never get to hear the audible voice of God. Most of the time, He speaks through the mind and feelings but I have to warn you to be careful in discerning the voice of God. God reveals and the devil reveals. One has to be careful which voice to trust because if it is not of God it will destroy your life and will be deviated from your destiny and be deceived to thinking that you were on the right path. Always check and ask questions to be sure that it is of the Lord – this is not to say you should doubt God but it will make a whole lot of difference in your Christian walk. Also, seek guidance from mature Christians and listen to prophecies about some of these things objectively.

Humility

Humility is a key factor for growing in the anointing. You must recognize the fact that it is the Lord himself who gives you the anointing as Apostle Paul wrote, "for who makes you differ from another? And what do you have that you did not receive? Now if you did receive it, why do you boast as if you had not received it?" (1 Cor 4:7). Since God is the giver of the anointing, He expects you to value it and treat it with respect. If you recognize that it is someone's power put at your disposal then you must use it as a good steward with great respect to the owner. "Who then is a faithful and wise servant, whom his master made ruler over his household, to give the food in due season? Blessed is that servant whom his master, when he comes, will find so doing. Assuredly, I say to you that he will make him ruler over all his goods. But if that evil servant says in his heart, my master is delaying his coming, and begins to beat his fellow servants, and to eat and drink with the drunkards, the master of that servant will come on a day when he is not looking for him and at an hour that he is not aware of, and will cut him in two and appoint him his portion with the hypocrites, there will be weeping and gnashing of teeth" (Matt 24:45-51). Therefore, God just makes you a steward of His power, which is the anointing, and you must give account of it. If you give a good account of yourself at the work then He will add to what He has given you and increase your anointing. If not, you will lose what you have. The Lord, his Spirit and His Angels know how to use the things of God. If you do not humble yourself, they will not teach or help you. That is why the apostles wrote, "For I say, through the grace given to me, to everyone who is among you, not to think of himself more highly than he ought to think, but to think soberly, as God has dealt to each one a measure of faith." (Rom. 12:3).If you want to grow in the anointing you must humble yourself to learn. As you humble yourself, you will be taught by those ahead and knowledgeable so that you can grow and improve in the anointing. Until you are willing to put aside arrogance and pride, you cannot progress to the next level.

Learning

The journey of growing in the anointing is a process of learning. When God gives you his anointing, it is up to you to learn, discover other uses and know the limits of the anointing, Everything of God is eternal so if you receive his power there is no end to the power available to you but He gives you limits to the power He permits you to wield as you grow in the anointing and maturity and responsible behavior, He enlarges the burdens of the power. In fact when the angel told Daniel about the age of power demonstration, also described it as an age of learning "knowledge shall increase.......but the people who know their God will be strong and do exploits" (Dan.11:32). Therefore, the knowledge of God is what produces the exploits. The greater knowledge of God the greater the exploits. That is why the apostle Paul prayed for the church "what do you not know, you do not believe and what do not believe, you cannot have. You can only know when you are enlightened and it is the Spirit of God that reveals it to us, or other Godly men tell us just as the Bible is doing." Eph 1:17-19. You must learn like an apprentice learns the trade to be able to practice the trade or like a trainee driver must learn how to drive and both written and unwritten laws on the road, that is how the anointing is. The anointing is a world on its own, so if you do not learn the things of that world you will fail. As you learn about the anointing and its usefulness, you will understand it better and it will grow just as you will grow in it and master how to use it and make impact.

Discipline

To be effective in the anointing and grow in the anointing, we must be disciplined. Apostle Paul wrote "but I discipline my body and bring it to subjection, least, when I have preached to others, I myself should become disqualified" 1 Cor. 9:27 to be quicker and better in the anointing, you must remove whatever baggage that will slow you down "let us lay aside every weight and sin which so easily ensnares us, and let us run with endurance the race that is set before us," Heb. 12:1 Jesus said "every branch in me that does not bear fruit he takes away; and every branch that bears fruit he prunes, that it may bear more fruit" John15:2 so how disciplined you are helps you to be productive. If you are not disciplined, your energy is dissipated but if you are focused, you become more productive. Discipline which is pruning, qualifies you to receive more grace or anointing from the Lord hence you grow in the anointing. The essence of God giving you anointing is to touch lives but how well organized you are can determine how many lives you touch and how effectively that are touched. Since God is orderly it is easier for Him to work with orderly people, so he will trust you with more grace. Let us study a few of the areas that need to be disciplined

Emotions

You have to be emotionally disciplined, you must have stable emotions, not high and low alternately. Because you must have emotional strength to meet the challenges of the life of an anointed person, the kind of emotions that pervade around you create an environment around you for the anointing to work or not to work and grow. Spiritual things work through emotions, the things of God be it anointing, power, angels or the Spirit of God like joyful environments, happy people and loving environment. The Lord commanded that "Jesus said to him "you shall love the Lord your God with all your heart, with al your soul, and with all your mind" Matt 22:37 you must therefore get a grip on your emotions and let only the emotions that are vital for the things of God to grow. In Gal. 5 we are told about the different kinds of fruits of the Spirit that your emotions generate and I believe before you receive a fruit, it is cultivated. So you must cultivate the fruits of the Spirit or you will get the fruits of the flesh as weeds in the farm and the fruit of the Spirit as fruits in the farm and your emotional life is the farm. If you do not cultivate the seeds of the fruit of the Spirit, then the seeds will be overgrown and choked by the weeds, which is the plants of the flesh and produce the fruit of the flesh. Every Spiritual thing the Lord gives is a seed as you cultivate it, it grows and becomes a giant tree." Another parable he put forth to them, saying the Kingdom of heaven is like a mustard seed which a man took and sowed in his field, which is indeed the least of all seeds, but when it is grown it is greater that the herbs and becomes a tree, so that the birds of the air come and nest in its branches" Matt. 13:31-32 so as you work hard on your emotions and try to remove the fruits of the flesh and nourish the seed of the Spirit of God, you will end up bearing the fruits of the Spirit. It is not an easy work but it will help you in the long run to grow in the anointing. To nourish the emotional seeds of God, you must follow the pattern Apostle Paul gave, " rejoice in the Lord always. Again I will say recjoice: let your gentleness be known to all men, the Lord is at hand. Be anxious for nothing, but in everything by prayer and supplication, with thanksgiving, let your requests be made known to God; and the peace of God which passes all understanding, will guard your hearts and mind through Christ Jesus. Finally, bretheren, what ever things are true, whatever things are lovely, whatever things are of good report, if there is anything praiseworthy- meditate o these things" Phil. 4:4-8 so by meditation on the things of good emotions and conscious effort to generate good emotions and asking the Lord to help you, you become a bearer of good fruit ' as a man thinketh in his heart so is he"Prov 23:7 your emotional body is your battery, it gives you drive and motivation, it generates enthusiasm and the energy for living the God kind of life. if you do not discipline and prune your emotions, you will not be fruitful in the area of interest to God and you will not have the right motivation to do the work, so God finds pruning it important.

Spirit

Your Spirit must be trained " the Spirit of a man will sustain in sickness, but who can bear a broken Spirit" Prov.18:14" a merry heart does good, like medicine, but a broken Spirit dries the bones" Prov.17:22. so having Spiritual strength sustains you to carry bigger anointing which involves bigger Spiritual responsibility. If you do not have a strong Spirit, you cannot go through the challenges involved in being anointed. So it is necessary to discipline and train your Spirit to be able to work in higher levels of Spiritual power. The higher you grow in Spiritual power, the more powerful and stronger the demons you meet. So if you cannot match them you are finished for that level. One Spiritual blow can kill you or bring you down. If you are also stronger and powerful it will not affect you. The only way to be strong spiritually is to grow in prayer and develop an aggressive Spirit. Though some people have naturally a strong spirit, for most people it has to be developed by practice and exercise. The stronger your spirit, the bigger your ability to undertake stronger opposition. The major weakness is fear, if you fear you become unable to defeat the demon before you, but as your Spirit becomes stronger you lose fear of certain levels of demons and you gain the confidence to operate in the realms of the Spirit. which in turn makes you more effective as a minister and the greater your level of recognition and respect in the spirit realm, the easier it becomes to work in the Spiritual realm. The work of ministry is a Spiritual work so you need spiritual stamina to do it. Just act anytime you are dreaming or seeing a vision try to be alive and be part of what you see and when you are attacked in your dreams try to fight back. the spirits of most people are sleeping so it is time to wake up Spiritually and take up who you are to be in the Spirit.

Health

Your body is the temple of the Spirit of God, so if it is not watched, you will be of no good in the long term. You are the physical representative of God by the anointing. if you do not watch your health, you will die and all the anointing will be of no use. So you must watch your health and maintain a healthy lifestyle and body.

Your mind

You need a developed mind, a mind that can understand the things of God and handle issues to life in ways that are best. The devil and demons we face have high intelligence, so if you do not have a trained and developed mind, they will always deceive you and get control of your mind, you should be quick to see through the wiles of the demons and handle them. You also need to discipline your mind so that it does not become a playground for the devil because your mind controls your life, it determines your steps and decisions. so if you do not control you mind, demons will pass all kinds of thoughts to your mind and eventually control you. So you must be careful what you allow your mind to do because it must be disciplined. as your mind is disciplined and groomed, it will become an asset and will help you in the work. So apostle Paul taught us "do not be conformed to this world, but be transformed by the renewing of your mind, that you may prove what is that good and acceptable and perfect will of God" Rom.12:2. which means, you must change the attitude of your mind, "that you put off, concerning your former conduct, according to deceitful lusts, and be renewed in the Spirit of your mind" Eph. 4:22-23 you must therefore make a definite effort to change your thinking and determine to be a better person, pleasing to the Lord. So you put his laws in your mind and let that be the foundation upon which you build your actions and as your mind becomes disciplined, it will begin to produce the right thoughts and make the right decisions. As you discipline your mind to study the word of God, it will change because your mind is rubbing with the mind of God. it is not so specific as being a copy of what the Bible says but to grow in its way is to flow in the wavelength of God's mind.

So the studying and understanding of the Bible helps you to think as a son of God, so it is a process of mental development into the nature of Christ. it is not being a repeat of the Bible but rather grasping the mind of the God who wrote the Bible. It helps your mind to understand the mind of God, so that you know exactly what the Lord wants. This is a lifelong journey and the Lord will help you in this journey.

Accountability

Everything the Lord gives us is according to our ability, so if we must receive more, we must prove that we have the capacity and capability to handle more of what he has given us. This leads to the need for accountability." Luke 19:12-26" "for he that is faithful in little shall be ruler over much" and to him to whom much is given much is required ." as you give a good account of yourself in the stewardship of the anointing given you, God adds more to you then you are able to do more things and carry greater responsibilities with God. so your level of anointing is based upon your level of proven ability to handle the responsibilities that the Lord has given you, and how well you can accomplish divine assignments, the more the Lord is impressed by your records and good account of yourself in handling what he has given you. He will give you more flexibility and allow you more anointing to operate in other areas and in higher levels. Because anointing is a responsibility, if you do not use it for your task, you will not grow in it. I must draw your attention to the fact that every anointing no matter how small or big are for specific assignments. Therefore, if you do not use it to accomplish the specific purpose, you have failed no matter what God used you to do, so you will not rise in the anointing. In God there is no shortcut even if God destined you for a great anointing, you must pass through the paths and challenges he has set before you. It is only after you give a good account of your self that you get promoted by God. "Rom. 14;12 " God judges our capabilities before giving us great responsibilities and great anointing. So every highly anointed man of God has proven himself time and time again to be effective or if not such a person will not last long with that anointing. There are things you do not take for granted at certain levels of anointing or it will cost you. At times it is not easy to be favored by God to carry big anointing because there are consequences, sacrifices to make challenges to overcome and serious accounts to give which others at lower levels will take for granted and go unpunished.

Spiritual Warfare

Your anointing is a weapon that God has given you to snatch people out of the hand of their enemies who are stronger than them. And also to strengthen, equip, empower people to accomplish their God given destinies. Is. 61:1-4 the anointing is given to you to release the power of God into human lives and also enforce the will of God in the affairs of men. For this reason you already have an adversary the devil, who does not want anything of God to happen to the lives of people and who is seeking to destroy you if you lose your Guard 1Pet. 5:8-10 he believes that if you smite the shepherd the sheep will scatter. So he will work harder to smite you the anointed more than the others. In fact every Christian is anointed because of Christ but those who are specifically assigned by the Lord to be channels of the anointing are targeted more. It is the duty of anointed ones to fend of these attacks and make sure the channel of the anointing is open, so the children of God will be blessed. The work anointed people have to do is to keep fighting as the devil keeps attacking so Apostle Paul wrote "Eph. 6:12" so we wrestle with Spiritual forces and push the away, God permits it because as the apostle Paul said "we must through much tribulation enter into the Kingdom of God " Acts14:22 God wants the demons of your level of anointing to recognize you that you are more than them so he will permit them to afflict you and you must fight them until you have come to a point of recognition as it happened in Acts19:15. Spiritual warfare is part of growing in the anointing because it gives you recognition. I also must emphasize that as you use your weapon of the anointing against the devil, he will also throw his at you. God will not hold the devil for you to just throw punches at him, it is going to be hit and I hit you back until one is down; but God gave us assurance that he will give us the all we need to win if we want to win and stand long enough. It also means that your anointing is worth nothing until you conquer your enemies with it. It is just like having the best weapons of war and allowing your enemies to invade and take your country because you did not use it. The anointing is to be used as you defeat your opposition, you are recognized and your sphere of influence is increased and then your dominion over demons is increased. I must also sound a note of caution, every anointing and the level of demons it can conquer. A lot of young and immature Christians just go about picking unnecessary Spiritual battles at times with demons stronger than themselves and so get into trouble and destroy or delay their Spiritual careers in the anointing. The greater the battles you fight, the slower your progress will be. And if you get into a fight with a demon far stronger than you, it will hold you prisoner until God has mercy on you and saves you or you fight till you are finally able to overcome it with God's help. So I advise that attack a demon that attacks you and nothing else or a demon that stands in your way determined to block you. That is why there are some cases some ministers cannot handle because their anointing is not up to that level. I have had my fair share of these mistakes so will not like someone to also fall into them. When I was young I stood on the scripture 'you are more than conquerors" and did strange kinds of warfare above my level and the repercussions were serious and damage huge some it has taken me about ten years to come out of some of those Spiritual revenge attacks, so I am talking from experience. There is a difference between zeal and knowledge, the essence of Spiritual growth is to gain Spiritual depth, knowledge and maturity and understanding. Every level of anointing you grow to, the demons of that level will try you and as you defeat them, they will come to gradually respect you and fear you and will not oppose you again. Therefore, when you speak it happens for that level without struggles. So it seems effortless but it comes after convincingly defeating demons that will attack you. The anointing increases after every win till it is full. If a demon attacks you, he exerts his power to counter your anointing so as your defeat him the number of demons opposing the free flow of the anointing is reduced by one until it comes to a level where as you keep defeating them one by one the force of the anointing on you increases to an extent that the group left holding you are overwhelmed.

So then your anointing flows without opposition because they have been conquered. Spiritual warfare also stretches your anointing , this enables you to know the limits of your anointing as the same time discover hidden potential of your anointing. it is only in Spiritual battles that you discover things that the anointing can help you to do and the kind of weapons the anointing makes available to you and what powers your anointing puts at your disposal. So Spiritual warfare helps you develop skill in the use of your anointing and capabilities. The most dangerous thing in Spiritual warfare you must watch out is demonic deception, that is why some men of God claim they are Elijah etc. which apostle Paul wrote"we are not ignorant of his devices" the Spirit of divination is very notorious for such. It portrays itself as the Spirit of God, or angels of God and give visions and speak. Which can make a genuine prophet false and a genuine teacher false. "1 John 2:18-19' if fact you must know the difference in which case it is an inner knowing. To see visions of angels in white or brightness does not mean it is from God and it is not every voice that claims to be God's that is from God so learn to read through the deception of demons in higher levels of Spiritual warfare. So try and check and be sure you are not deceived and then not mislead yourself and others into the trap of demons.

Respect for superiors

What you do not respect you cannot have, what you do not value you cannot nurture to grow and you will not receive it. Iron sharpens iron and whosoever walks with the wise shall be wise. So the people you associate with and respect will have a profound effect on your life and as you submit to a superior, what is upon his life will be gradually over time be imparted or transferred to you. This is the essence of fellowship with the Lord in prayer as you keep submitting and respecting and serving the Lord, the Lord gradually imparts something in your life. As you respect the ministry of someone ahead of you, his anointing gradually in increasing measure rubs into your life and upon you. That is why those how serve a man of God will get a part of, if not all his gifts. As you humble your self and honor your senior minister, his anointing is gradually poured on you; it can grow so much that you might look like a carbon copy of him. That is why it is important to respect and honor your pastor or his anointing will not benefit you as a church member, as some people complain that they are not being blessed in his church, but they forget that they don't respect him but condemn and find faults of him all the time. The ideal of such a relationship was between Moses and Joshua, Elijah and Elisha. in such cases the servant receives what his master has and carries on his work with no vacuum left.

The biggest problem of today is anointed ministers die with their anointing, people are not inheriting their anointing, so Spiritual positions that they occupied to hold the devil at bay becomes vacant as they die and demons take over and Christians lose Spiritual ground. In this age where everybody thinks he can have his own anointing I want to make it clear that in God's Kingdom, God chooses who should have what but someone who will otherwise have little anointing are given the privilege of receiving the anointing of some one bigger by inheritance which comes by faithful service so they can build on that anointing and take it further. Elisha did more miracles then his master and he did not have to fight Spiritual battles to establish his authority because it was already there. The Lord once told me that he does not need anointing in heaven so men of God should try to leave the anointing for another to continue and improve the work. Instead of dying with it and letting the whole process of gaining Spiritual ground start again when in fact they can be consolidated and enlarged if the anointing and mantles were passed on to someone else to continue after their death. And those under the men of God should serve well and not disrespect them and expect to receive anything or even the devil will laugh at you as a hypocrite and that you don't deserve it. We need more anointing here to help push the devil further backwards so that the new ones God releases will not struggle much but gain speed and back up the ones down here and build upon that thereby increasing the potency of all the other anointing.

CHAPTER FOUR
PAYING THE PRICE

"We must go through many hardships to enter the Kingdom of God" (Acts 14:22). There comes a time in your journey to your anointing that no prayer seems to work, and all your efforts seem to fail. That is the time you are paying the price of the anointing. You pay the price especially through the work you do, the obstacles you face, the challenges we have to overcome, and the attacks the devil throws at you. This makes you worthy of the anointing; all these sum up as the price you pay to carry your anointing. If you pay the price, the anointing is yours. If you do not pay the price, the anointing is borrowed and you can lose it. Some one once said that the anointing is heavens treasure. If it is heaven's treasure in earthen vessels as apostle Paul called it 2 Cor. 4:7, then how much are you willing to pay for it. Like the parable of Jesus about the Kingdom "Matt. 13:44-46" in each of these parables the seekers sold all, in fact, gave up everything to have that one treasure; and are you also willing to sacrifice all, go through everything to acquire the anointing. What God does is to give a shadow of the anointing to operate with - just a glimpse, then he asks the price from you. At times, God does not give you a glimpse but you pay the price before you receive it - He may give you prophesies about the anointing He is giving you to keep you going. And in some case, you pay a series of prices to grow into different levels of anointing until you get to the fullness of the anointing. However, God chooses the path for you before finally giving it to you in full. As you go on using it, you pay the price through mastering what you have . Paying the price brings the devil into play. If your anointing will be effective, the devil must accept and recognize you. This also means that the devil must (do all against you) try his best against you according to the level of anointing God is giving you. The devil also wants to prove that you do not deserve the anointing. Just as he, the devil, attempted to do against the high priest Joshua (Zech3:1-4) - so will he try to destroy your testimony before God until you are not fit to receive the anointing. If you do well to survive the attacks from the devil, then you will be honored with the anointing. Many potentially powerful men and women of God do not amount to anything in their lives as servants of God because they did not pay the price for the anointing. They either did not have the courage to step out and claim what God called them to be or they could not defeat the strategies of the devil employed to bring them down. They did not persevere or push hard enough; they did not stand up and refused to be brought down by the problems that the devil sent their way. The devil will do everything to prevent your anointing from coming through and from making impact. He will do every thing to prevent the ministry from taking off. He can also bring unfaithful workers to frustrate the work with crises and problems. He can even direct you to a wrong wife or wrong husband. there are certain women who can handle the responsibilities of a pastor wife by nature and some women are also willing to learn and change for such roles but in these days when men are attracted by beauty, a lot of young ministers fall into this trap and then strange women can be sent to also make a man of God fall by building a soul tie and seeping away his anointing or create problems. At times, the price of the anointing is what you have to contend with because of what you have it is not because you are going to receive but rather because you received. Therefore, they will fight you to steal your anointing to prevent it from coming to light. Jesus was fought by the devil not because Jesus was going to be the Son of God but rather because he was the Son of God. Job was fought because of the blessing the Lord had granted him. the apostles paid the price by facing intimidation beatings etc. they went through it not to earn the anointing but rather they went through it because of what God had given them, it was the process for the physical actualization of it so the price is the obstacles and challenges you have overcome to make it a physical reality. Another side to the price of the anointing is the responsibility it brings like Moses coming to a point of despair by the troubles of the people, how well you maintain and handle it will determine how effective your anointing will be . in short the price to the anointing is the responsibility of using the anointing and the attacks that the devil and his agents will throw at you because of the anointing you have en granted. So it brings the two dimensions of the anointing. God ward and the devil ward, God will expect you to be trained to be able to effectively and efficiently discharge the responsibilities of the anointing and the higher the anointing, the more rigorous and demanding the training. At the same time the devil will consistently attack you to make sure you do not finish your training to receive the anointing so he will torment and torture you till you give up the whole idea of being anointed. So you get caught up with two opposing forces at work to bring the best out of you so that you can make impact and survive the pressure of the work before you. For most of the anointed men of God, your destinies are given by God but there is always a meeting of the courts of heaven and the devil being a son of God, is a member and in this meetings the challenges and obstacles and standards are set for every individual, they need to see if

1. You really desire that level of anointing.
2. How much are you willing to sacrifice for it, so the question is how much is the anointing worth to you
3. How strong are you to carry the anointing that is about to be granted
4. How responsible are you such that you will not abuse and misuse the powers of the office the anointing gives you
5. How far are you willing to go for the work of God
6. Your interests and motivation behind what you are seeking
7. Your organizational ability

I want you to beware that the fact that you get dreams about the anointing and ministry does not mean you will have it or you have the anointing. What God is doing most of the time is just asking you if you will like to have it. The truth is that it happens for most blessings. If you seek the anointing and start to desire after if then the price is set for you to pay. For some the anointing is given to them before they were born, for some they have a choice to honor the call of the anointing or not. If just follows the pattern of Rom. 8:28-30. God predestines an anointing for you and calls you to it, if you decide to answer the call; then every step you take towards the anointing is the process of justification in which you overcome many things to get to the place of the anointing and when you get to that place because you have been proved and approved, God glorifies you by giving you the anointing. There are two angles to price paying for the anointing. The first is the obstacles and challenges you must face and overcome to get the anointing and the sacrifices and choices you must make to receive the anointing. The second angle is the duties and responsibilities you have to do or carry to maintain the anointing. If you do not protect and nurture what God has given you, you can lose it. For example Samson lost his anointing for some time once his hair was cut the anointing left for a season and he was powerless until his hair grew back. Therefore, each way there is a price to pay. Keeping the anointing is a very demanding business. It means perfect obedience and constant nurturing of the anointing. There are different kinds if anointing but they can operate at the same level or Spiritual position of power so the prices also varies for each one. For example there is a teaching anointing that goes with a teaching ministry, a prophetic anointing which makes for prophecy, miracle anointing that produces miracles, deliverance anointing for deliverance, healing anointing for healing etc. so it is very important that you know the kind of anointing that is coming, and because of the work that the anointing will do. You must be trained to be able to effectively use that anointing, which is also a price you will pay for anointing. Some anointing brings you in conflict with Satanic forces more than others and in such a case the Lord will make you experience The devil at work first hand so you know what you will be dealing with and the level of anointing also determines the intensity and seriousness of your experience. if it will be at higher levels of Spiritual power, you will be contending with higher levels of demons and in such a case God will expose you to the kind of attacks such higher demons do in your life so that when you are at work with the anointing you know them and what they can do and what you must do. In such a case God gives you the grace. " no one can receive anything except it is given to him from above" ask any one God has put in direct conflict with Satan himself or higher demonic forces and he or she will tell you it is not easy. So if God does not grant you that grace you will not survive it. This demons are wiser, quicker and more effective and the resources and network of demons at their disposal is more so they can make your life hell. They can set you up and block anything from happening in your life. Price paying can be dangerous that is why Jesus said" many are called but few are chosen" not everybody is able to pay the price and persevere enough to receive the anointing," Heb. 10:37-39" so paying the price is a demanding Endeavour but it will finally reward you with all that anointing can give and bring you.

You must know that the anointing makes you a servant of a master God and the anointing is the equipment and the seal of the authority to do the work. So God also depends upon your total obedience, so that he can expect you to do exactly as he wants it done and in the way he wants. The price of the anointing includes learning obedience because you are empowered to represent the Lord. So there is very little room for error because you must not miss those little direction which are critical to the work just as Jesus went through to be able to do his work effectively. Heb. 5:7-10 God did not say because he was a son, he was exempted from going through the sufferings that bring obedience. There are certain things that the only way to learn it is to suffer it. You must realize that concerning the work of God the ultimate is absolute obedience. Because at times the obedience to that little direction will make the difference between life and death for someone God want to reach or healing and deliverance for another and if you do not obey that window of opportunity is missed and that person might never get another chance in his or her lifetime. So one of the things God teaches you is obedience. The higher the level of anointing and work he is giving you, the higher the level of tests and trials to improve your obedience level, because most of the things God sends his servants to do are demanding. In as much as God sent Moses to pharaoh, each opposition Moses faced was also to prove his level of obedience and when he had earned it as thefaithful in all the Lord's house, nobody had a right to oppose Moses. As people grow in obedience there are some commandments the Lord gives which are not necessary but they are vital in proving if you will obey the Lord whatever the cost. When God wanted to test the level of obedience of king Saul he used a trivial issue the Lord told him to kill everything he saw in the land of amalek 1 Sam. 15. the sparing of the sheep and the life of agag the amalek king was not really an issue but what the Lord required was that, will he put his self interest aside and do what the Lord says like we read in Ps.15:4". In serving the Lord, it is not a matter of doing things at your convenience, it is being totally surrendered to your master's service. Can the Lord be sure to trust you that you will always be at his disposal and be useful. If you are not useful to God, he will not use you. And to be useful, you need to be totally surrendered to his will, so that he can send you to do things on his behalf. As you go through these fires of trial, you develop a deep understanding of the issues of your calling. That is why God sends people to be mentored by others ahead of them in the field that he wants to use them so that you will learn in practice the important issues that pertain to your calling. Your character will be tested for character flaws, any flaws can cost you in this journey into a greater anointing. If you do not exhibit godly character that is pleasing to God, the giver of the anointing, he will not give it to you. Since the anointing is what God gives you to operate in a certain Spiritual level, you will have to earn your respect in that Spiritual level. You must understand that Spiritual lifting is a promotion by God to operate in a higher Spiritual level and anointing is what God gives you to operate in that level. Therefore, the Spiritual powers of that level will fight you to dispossess you of the anointing so that you cannot operate in that level, which means they have sacked you from that level. As far as God is concerned he has given it to you, you will have to fight and reclaim it or live with the effect of that defeat all your life. If you cannot win in one level then you cannot go to the next level. Anointing comes from God and he determines when to give and what quantity to give, he determines what price you shall pay to receive and keep an anointing. When God gives the anointing he has given, and it is only a matter of time before it shows. The price of the anointing is what you have to contend with because of what you have, it is not because you are going to receive but rather because you have received so the enemy will fight you to steal your anointing to prevent it from coming to light. Every anointing you will receive is already determined and given by God, he will then show you a picture or vision of it or tell you about it. And God determines the things you must go through to receive it, it could be training and persecution like David. Every anointed person must go through wilderness experiences like Moses that is the time you find God and develop your character for your destiny on earth. For some it is staying in obscurity and learning from others before you are released by God to operate in your anointing. For some it is Spiritual warfare etc. there are certain things you go through or happen to you just because you are anointed and that is the price. Winston Churchill once said that "the price of greatness is responsibility" there are certain things, responsibilities, problems, attacks, criticisms, disgrace, etc. that will come your way because you are anointed of God and that is the price you pay. For Paul the apostle he had to kill himself daily so that he will not be proud and carry the burden of preaching the gospel because he was anointed, Jeremiah had to prophesy against his people because of the anointing on his life. Elijah had to stand against Israel and jezebel because of the anointing, Ezekiel had to lie one side of his body for some days, another prophet had to walk in sackcloth for some time. All these things are unpleasant things but they had to do them because of the anointing on their life, that is the price they paid. Another price that any anointed servant pays is obedience to God in the case of strong opposition, the whole world does not agree and support you but you are standing on that decision because God said so. Trials are part of the life of an anointed man or woman of God because the devil will always be finding ways to bring him down. That is what an anointed person will have to live with. Everything of God has a price there is nothing free in this Kingdom. If you do not pay the price you cannot permanently keep it. A lady was called by God into the ministry of solving marital problems, and for that assignment she had to go through problems in her marriage for almost ten years before it stopped. After that, God released her into that ministry. For my anointing , I have had to go through years of no progress in life and ministry, there was a time that for three years I had only four constant members and no matter the amount of evangelism and prayer, all new souls kept leaving as they came. At the same time I was forced to defeat different kinds of demonic powers who were determined to close down my ministry. The things I went through and battles I fought has helped me to know how demonic powers operate and how to defeat them if I meet such cases. So my ten years of wilderness in ministry was training for anointing. I have experienced breakaways and my has ministry collapsed many times, I have suffered much disgrace and afflictions because the devil was using his resources to prevent my anointing and assignment from coming to fruition. I have seen different kinds of demons of higher rank even the queen of the sea and the devil himself and I have survived their attacks, i have had to earn my respect and authority so that they can say they know me, as the mad man said "Jesus I know, Paul I know'. the apostle was right when he wrote that he shared the sufferings, he had endured to carry the Gospel as far as he had reached 2 Cor11:23-12:6. the devil and his people will try you with temptations, afflictions, threats, suffering, obstacles etc just to stop you. But the painful thing is after all these suffering some people never see the light of the anointing. For some, they did not understand their place and calling. For some, they were in the wrong location, for instance if God called and sent you to China and you are in the United Kingdom doing ministry you will never shine. If you are to be a head pastor and you work as associate minister because you do not want to start your ministry you will never see your anointing producing fruit but rather you will always have problems with your head, Because you are out of your place of destiny. If you are also to be under someone you will not shine if you are on your own, until you are in order with God. So discovering the purpose of the your anointing and where you are to be located is part of the price you pay. In paying the price, you also discover the size of your anointing and what you can do and not do with it. The devil wants to prove to the Lord that you do not deserve the anointing and try to steal it from you because if you value the anointing you will not lose it. Many potentially powerful men and woman of God did not anoint to everything in their life because they did not pay the price. They either did not step out to claim what God called them to be, or they could not defeat the strategies of the enemies. Some got married to wrong partners so their marriage was a weight of stone that tied them down. Some did not persevere or push hard enough. Some also did not stand up and refuse to be brought down by the problems the devil sent on their way. Overcome everything the devil throws at you to prove to God that you want the anointing. Some of the strategies he will use is unfaithful workers, he will bring people that will not do the work but rather spoil it. Bad partners and manipulation of your partner to make bad choices and take a bad actions. he could also work to isolate you by destroying your credibility that is why scandals happen To the genuine ministers at times. it might be a small issue that is common to life but it will be blown to huge proportions. He can send series of failures your way, it becomes as if everything you do fails and you do not make progress in anything then added to that, disappoints and frustrations just to make you give up. There are 3 ways to pay the price depending on the will of God.

1. some pay the price in full before the anointing appears
2. For some a grandfather has paid the price or ancestor, mother or family members in a previous generation, such people do not suffer much in the ministry.
3. For some the price is paid as the move into each level so in such cases the price is paid then you move into a new level of anointing. It is as Paul said, "I die daily" a continuous price was being paid in his life.

It can happen that for some it is a combination of those three ways or just two of the ways but it is all dependent on the will of God concerning his purpose concerning the anointing.

The price

God is looking at in paying the price some key things.

1. Relationship with God –

there are three people you can have relationship with the Father, the Son and the Holy Spirit. But you must realize is that the Father is the overall and the reserves the right to permit the Son and the Spirit to get close to you. So if you please the father he can allow or deeper intimacy of the son and the Spirit. Having a relationship with the father is important the deeper your relationship, the deeper your relationship will be with the son and the Spirit. I must make you aware that each of the three have their individuality, character, preference, and nature as you get closer to them you will learn the difference among them. Your relationship with God is critical because it is because of your relationship with the Lord, that the anointing is released. Everyone must grow in their relationship with the Lord but in the case of some people, their parents or grandparents have laid their foundation. Therefore, if you are dealing with God, you must work hard because you are laying a foundation for generations after you. for those whose parents have laid the foundation, they do not struggle to start their relationship with the Lord and also they grow faster in their walk with the Lord. There are certain privileges they enjoy and they suffer less for what the Lord gives them and for gifts that the Lord grants.

2. Spiritual background-

Spiritual background is very necessary in your Spiritual walk, " if the foundation is destroyed there is nothing the righteous can I do". I recently met some friends with whom we started ministry at the same time, we all had a genuine and sincere desire to serve the Lord, but of the whole group I was the only one left who was still pursuing this course of ministry. they had quit ministry and had gone into other vocations and had prospered, they said that it is not that they did not want to serve the Lord but they were getting to a point that they were getting disgraced. They saw no progress in their life and it was as if no matter how hard they prayed God there Was not a change their situation. I understood it and I knew why, it was our spiritual background and I was sure our suffering will have no been that much and we will have excelled earlier and quicker if we knew in those days we started. It was because of his pagan background that God spoke to Abraham to leave his family and go to an unknown place to be able to establish a relationship with him. I do not know why but God always expects us to break free from our background by demonstrating in practical term a genuine desire to be free before he delivers us. "Whosoever calls upon the name of the Lord shall be saved" but as to the time he will come and save you is up to him. When God came to work with Gideon he asked him to destroy their family shrine and destroy the idols. It has always been a pattern of the Lord, that before he came to save his people he demanded that they confess their sins break every contact with idols, before he stepped in with blessing. This is the concept behind generational blessings and curses. When God said to the Hebrews that" you shall have no other gods before me" Ex. 20:3, he meant it and wanted no competition.

He can show you his plan for your life but he will not completely step in until these other gods have been dispatched from our life. God expects us to remove any ties with demonic gods in our bloodline. In the west these things are not much of an issue , since over time generation after generation of families have overcome it and devoted themselves to the Lord. In some of these generations, they have received revivals, those major moves of God broke the hold of demons over many families, but in Africa, it has not been so most of the time. The person the anointing is falling upon is a first generation of the family, to encounter God which means the demonic powers that control the family will punish you and attack you to give up that foreign god you have brought into the family and since most people have not renounced the works of darkness. It is most probably that you will live in an environment controlled by demonic forces. You even meet cases where anointed men of God are not making progress in the ministry because they are married to woman who practice the dark art of witchcraft, until these holds of Satan are broken you will not be free. Some people have parents who have strong ties with demon gods. I once dealt with a case of a Christian sister, very dynamic and gifted by the Lord but no matter how hard she prayed and fasted and worked hard She was not making progress. when we dealt with her background, we discovered that she was named after her grandmother who happened to be a worshipper of a thunder god so the god had a hold on her because of the background link to her grandmother after that hold was broken she began to make progress in life. I have dealt with many cases of anointed people who were not making progress because of their background. So it is important to correct your background to be able to make relevant progress in the anointing.

3. Competence in handling the power and gift-
the responsibility of being anointed by God and given power and gifts to use is competence. How competent are you in handling these gifts and power, it takes time to understand your gifts how they operate and the power that God has given you. You must develop competence or you will misuse your anointing and destroy others. Competence is developed by facing challenges and spending time in seclusion to be taught of God. This leads us to the wilderness experience that is common to anybody who has been anointed by God. Moses had to be in the wilderness of Sinai tending sheep to learn how to shepherd the flock of God and also the whole Sinai area well to be able to lead the Israelites there from Egypt and also discover himself and develop a reliance on God and develop the stillness in him to

hear the voice of God. The wilderness experience is important to God and he will send you to it as many times, as he wants to be able to have time alone with you to impart in you and build you for what is ahead of you. The wilderness experience is the time in the life of a person anointed by God when nothing happens in your life, but God keeps revealing himself to you and teaches you new things and imparts his powers into you to do the work that is ahead of you. Elijah had to go through the wilderness twice, at the time of famine and secondly after the mount Carmel encounter with the false prophets. So that he will know exactly what God wanted of him and do it. the wilderness is what you must go through to spend time with God without distractions so that he can impart in you what you need to excel in the work. it is after these experiences that you develop the confidence and competence in handling the power that has been given to you. It was during the wilderness experiences that enabled David to know the Lord better and to trust Him and hear his voice which helped him to stand out as a great leader and was able to set up the foundation to the state organized worship of God. these things cannot be done by a person who has not had a personal and intense relationship with the Lord. As apostle Peter once wrote "2 Pet1:16"xxxx, and apostle John also wrote '1 John1:1-3xxxx. they had tasted something so they shared, of what use is a messenger without a message. You can only have the passion to a cause, when you have seen the vision or had an encounter with the master to do his bidding. That makes you competent because you know what you are doing and why you are doing it. And you have a deep understanding which does not come from books and other peoples revelations but from within because the master has done his work in you and planted his seed in you in the wilderness to germinate and produce fruit for all to see. You will always know the difference between an anointed message and rhetoric of words if you have been through the wilderness of God. You will know what is of God and what is of flesh.

4. Spiritual recognition

" Jesus I know, Paul I know; but who are you" Acts 19:15 that is what the demon said of Paul and Jesus. What do demons say about you? It is only by consistent defeat of demons as they stand in your way that you gain recognition. That is what Paul meant by "Eph 6;12 and 2 Cor 10:3-6" he had consistently overcome challenges to his work. The gospel is a spiritual thing and any one who has not fought spiritually for it, has no business preaching it because you are a spiritual laughing-stock to Satan and his demons. Since light and darkness do not meet, Satan and demons will fight you to see if you can stand in that level of anointing you have been granted by the Lord. The anointing that you operate on if you are anointed by God, has a level and each level has demons that operate on that level so they will fight with you to make sure you do not enter there. That is the Spiritual warfare you face, do not go looking for Spiritual fights you will have plenty to fight to attain Spiritual recognition. For any Spiritual level of anointing you will have to contend with demons of that level till they accept you at that level. These spiritual battles are for your spiritual life and rank , if you do not win these battles you will not get your rank and the level the anointing the Lord has given you will not happen. So it is important to win your Spiritual battles to receive Spiritual recognition, as you defeat bigger and powerful demons that attack you, the recognition will come. do not go looking for fights that are not yours. In fact one of the first commandments that the Lord Jesus gave his disciples was to go and cast out devils. Every anointed man or woman must be able to cast out demons according to your level of anointing. Therefore, if you cannot cast out demons then it means you do not have spiritual weight. You must grow to be Spiritually recognized as you win your battles. You increase in rank until you reach the level of anointing that the Lord has given you.

5. Trust

If God can trust you, he will give you his power to use . There are times that the Lord will instruct you to do things that you do not understand. the truth is that he just wants to see how much you will go for him. How much will you sacrifice for the Lord? To serve the Lord is not all about sacrifice all the time. There comes a time the Lord blesses you, he gives you reward for your labour and suffering. he releases these blessings because he knows you have earned and deserve it. But you have to convince the Lord that he can trust you with his power and also how much you are willing to fight for his blessing or power in your life. To prove you are trustworthy, the Lord will let you go through challenges and demand sacrifices of you to be sure of you and also to earn you respect in the eyes of all just like Job. His commitment to God was trusted but tested so the devil held a series of challenges and sacrifices and his very will to serve the Lord was tested to see if his heart is true. A lot of times the only way to prove your heart is through hardship. a lot of people will claim that they love the Lord but will their love for the Lord stand when things go tough? Will they stand by their claim or change when they face disappointments? The Lord once asked me "what will you do if I fail you?" Will you still stand for the Lord who has failed you or delayed in coming? Then we will know that your heart is true to the Lord, the level of power that the Lord wants to grant you determines the seriousness of the hardship and challenges you will face to get to earn your right before the Lord and the hosts of heaven.

Sacrifice

Ps 50:1-5

The Mighty One, God the LORD,
Has spoken and called the earth
From the rising of the sun to its going down. 2 Out of Zion, the perfection of beauty,
God will shine forth. 3 Our God shall come, and shall not keep silent;A fire shall devour before Him, And it shall be very tempestuous all around Him. 4 He shall call to the heavens from above, And to the earth, that He may judge His people: 5 "Gather My saints together to Me, Those who have made a covenant with Me by sacrifice."

NKJV

Every sacrifice you make for God, improves your covenant with him as a servant, them more you have gone through for the sake of the gospel strengthens your position in the presence of God. How much of ugly service have you had to serve in the house of God or his ministers? These days people feel too big and are so rights conscious that they lose the anointing because the price has not been paid. Matt 16:24-25

Then Jesus said to His disciples, "If anyone desires to come after Me, let him deny himself, and take up his cross , and follow Me. 25 For whoever desires to save his life will lose it, but whoever loses his life for My sake will find it

NKJV

When you chose the path of sacrifice then you will get the anointing Heb 11:24-28

24 By faith Moses, when he became of age, refused to be called the son of Pharaoh's daughter, 25 choosing rather to suffer affliction with the people of God than to enjoy the passing pleasures of sin, 26 esteeming the reproach of Christ greater riches than the treasures in Egypt; for he looked to the reward.

27 By faith he forsook Egypt, not fearing the wrath of the king; for he endured as seeing Him who is invisible. 28 By faith he kept the Passover and the sprinkling of blood, lest he who destroyed the firstborn should touch them.

NKJV

The reason the people of the past were able to experience the anointing was because the were willing to sacrifice their comfort and pleasures to obey or chose to rather spend time with God that please people

Disgrace and humility

One painful price you pay for the anointing is disgrace and humility. It is not everytime that God commands you that obedience bring good results sometime in obedience you can rather suffer for obedience. If it happened to jesus how much more you the follower. Phil 2:5-11

Let this mind be in you which was also in Christ Jesus, 6 who, being in the form of God, did not consider it robbery to be equal with God, 7 but made Himself of no reputation, taking the form of a bondservant, and coming in the likeness of men. 8 And being found in appearance as a man, He humbled Himself and became obedient to the point of death, even the death of the cross. 9 Therefore God also has highly exalted Him and given Him the name which is above every name, 10 that at the name of Jesus every knee should bow, of those in heaven, and of those on earth, and of those under the earth, 11 and that every tongue should confess that Jesus Christ is Lord, to the glory of God the Father.

NKJV

The position of jesus was got by a painful affliction which happened because he was obeying the lord1 Peter 5:5-7

Likewise you younger people, submit yourselves to your elders. Yes, all of you be submissive to one another, and be clothed with humility, for

"God resists the proud,
But gives grace to the humble."

6 Therefore humble yourselves under the mighty hand of God, that He may exalt you in due time, 7 casting all your care upon Him, for He cares for you.

NKJV

The more you are humbled by serving people you think you are better then the more you improve your credentials with God. Such that you can be given greater anointing but if you are proud and cannot humble yourself the God will humble you and not give you anything Deut 8:2-3

2 And you shall remember that the LORD your God led you all the way these forty years in the wilderness, to humble you and test you, to know what was in your heart, whether you would keep His commandments or not. 3 So He humbled you, allowed you to hunger, and fed you with manna which you did not know nor did your fathers know, that He might make you know that man shall not live by bread alone; but man lives by every word that proceeds from the mouth of the LORD.

NKJV

As you go through disgrace and the develop humility then you will become a greatly anointed person the bible tells us that Moses even at his level of anointing was meek and was lowly as a result of which God was willing to fight anyone who opposed or disobeyed him. Heb 3:5

5 And Moses indeed was faithful in all His house as a servant, for a testimony of those things which would be spoken afterward,

NKJV

CHAPTER FIVE

MANTLES

In Ex. 28 the Lord specifically authorized Moses to make garments for Aaron the high priest and his sons. he had a reason for this "they shall be on Aaron and his sons when they come into the tabernacle of meeting, or when they come near the alter to minister In the holy place; that they do not incur iniquity and die. It shall be a statute forever to him and his descendants after him" Ex. 28:43 if you are called to serve by the Lord, he will give you a dress, which is called a mantle with which to go and serve. Just as every trade has a working gear. For instance construction workers have their helmet, boots and overalls that is how the principle of the mantles works. The mantle gives you delegated authority and right to do the work without being counter attacked and empowers you to be sharper and quicker in your gifting. It gives you special protection and recognition in the realm of the Spirit. Just as a police officer or soldier is a normal human being without the uniform but in the uniform, they have the power of the state backing them. That is what the mantle is. The mantle gives you the backing of heaven and declares to all that you are sent as a special messenger of God, to do the assignment of the Kingdom of heaven and everyone must give you the respect and cooperation. In addition, without the mantle you cannot stand before the Lord, like the parable of the great supper when those without the right garments were thrown out. I do not know all about the mantle yet but the mantle is given only to those called, chosen and anointed by God, the mantle is technically another level of power higher then the anointing reserved only for the ministers of God. Apostles, prophets, teachers, pastors, evangelists, etc. it gives you certain rights in coming before the Lord and work. It is not for every Christian but for the servants in the ministry. There are different kinds of mantles and they vary according to spiritual rank, area of calling and levels of access before the Lord. However, no two mantles are the same, but in very rare occasions you meet a person with multiple but they are a select few. Mantles are not common but they are given only to those called by God to do the work of the ministry, and may be passed on from a man of God to another to continue the work he was doing. The anointing empowers every believer because every believer can and must be anointed, but the mantle is given to servants of God for the work of the ministry. The anointing enables the believer to function as Mark16:17-18 and operate in the gifts of the Spirit, but the mantle gives the servants specialized areas of operation as the Lord calls them to service. If a servant of God is anointed, he operates the gifts of the Spirit and does the things promised by God to every believer, but if he receives a mantle, he is empowered to operate very effectively in the areas that the Lord called him. For example if he has a mantle of healing, he will heal at a level that excels all those anointed will not reach. It is a specialized thing, only for the minister. Work that is done without the mantle is ordinary but those done by the mantle are the lord's authority at work at high excellence. You can be anointed to flow in a certain area at a particular time but you have a mantle to operate in you area of calling. If you have a mantle you can do your calling, but the anointing will enable you to flow in a specific area if you are called in that area. 'He who is the high priest among his brethren, on whose head the anointing oil was poured and who is consecrated to wear the garments, shall not uncover his head nor tear his clothes;

NKJV Lev 21:10 As far as God is concerned, his servant is to have the anointing on his head and a mantle around him and must not be removed for any reason or else there will be punishment, because God has appointed his servant a chief of his people. Lev 21:3-4

4 Otherwise he shall not defile himself, being a chief man among his people, to profane himself.

NKJV

Mantles are very important in giving the laws to the priest God made it clear that no priest was ever to come into his presense to serve without wearing his attire of service the mantle in their case the priestly garments Ex 28:1-3

"Now take Aaron your brother, and his sons with him, from among the children of Israel, that he may minister to Me as priest, Aaron and Aaron's sons: Nadab, Abihu, Eleazar, and Ithamar. 2 And you shall make holy garments for Aaron your brother, for glory and for beauty. 3 So you shall speak to all who are gifted artisans, whom I have filled with the spirit of wisdom, that they may make Aaron's garments, to consecrate him, that he may minister to Me as priest.

NKJV without the mantle or garments the priests could not stand before the lord Ex 28:42-43

43 They shall be on Aaron and on his sons when they come into the tabernacle of meeting, or when they come near the altar to minister in the holy place, that they do not incur iniquity and die. It shall be a statute forever to him and his descendants after him.

NKJV if they did not have the mantle their ministry was ended they died. In our morden times it means that ministry will not be accepted by the lord and the ministry of that person will die. The mantle commissions you to work before the lord, you see that in the visions of Zachariah, in his vision he saw the high priest and because his garment was not clean the devil was opposing his ministry Zech 3:1-5

Then he showed me Joshua the high priest standing before the Angel of the LORD, and Satan standing at his right hand to oppose him. 2 And the LORD said to Satan,"The LORD rebuke you, Satan! The LORD who has chosen Jerusalem rebuke you! Is this not a brand plucked from the fire?"

3 Now Joshua was clothed with filthy garments, and was standing before the Angel.

4 Then He answered and spoke to those who stood before Him, saying, "Take away the filthy garments from him." And to him He said, "See, I have removed your iniquity from you, and I will clothe you with rich robes."

5 And I said, "Let them put a clean turban on his head."

So they put a clean turban on his head, and they put the clothes on him. And the Angel of the LORD stood by.

NKJV after he was dressed up in the mantle or garments he was commissioned. Gen 1:1 - Zech 3:10

Then the Angel of the LORD admonished Joshua, saying, 7 "Thus says the LORD of hosts:

'If you will walk in My ways, And if you will keep My command, Then you shall also judge My house, And likewise have charge of My courts; I will give you places to walk Among these who stand here.

8 'Hear, O Joshua, the high priest, You and your companions who sit before you, For they are a wondrous sign; For behold, I am bringing forth My Servant the BRANCH. 9 For behold, the stone That I have laid before Joshua: Upon the stone are seven eyes. Behold, I will engrave its inscription,' Says the LORD of hosts,' And I will remove the iniquity of that land in one day. 10 In that day,' says the LORD of hosts,' Everyone will invite his neighbor Under his vine and under his fig tree.'" NKJV the mantle is an extension of the anointing but it is a specialized form because it makes you function in an office, which others cannot because in the case of the mantle the bearer is the chief of that area.

You see the mantle in the life of Joseph as he was in the midst of his family; he was given a coat of many colors which set him apart from his brothers. when he was a slave in potifer's house he was made chief servant, in prison he was in charge of the prison and in the presence of pharaoh he was made prime minister. Another example of mantle at work is the life of Elisha at Jordan he received the mantle of his master Elisha and when he used the mantle to open the Jordan as his master did the sons of the prophets recognized that he was now the new chief of the prophets in the place of his master. He went on to heal the waters of jercho. One thing I believe you see in the life of Elisha concerning the mantle is that when you have the mantle to function in a certain area it just comes into action. When he was told about the problem of the waters of Jericho he just asked for the source of the water and salt and healed the water. Again, when the axe head fell in the water he only asked for where the axe fell and then he had immediate solution. These days the truth of the mantle is not understood because of that, we do not see men and women of God standing in the gap anymore and they do not have spiritual recognition. The unique thing about mantles is that they just quicken themselves when the need it was given for, arises and it is part of the servant of God so long as he lives a holy life and does not soil it. One thing I have personally learnt about a mantle is that when it is quickened you hear the voice of the lord clearer and sharper you see into the spirit better and you are very effective. You see the mantle is a form of the anointing but in the form of cloth in the life of Gideon, you see this as work Judg 6:33-34

34 But the Spirit of the LORD came upon Gideon; then he blew the trumpet, and the Abiezrites gathered behind him.

NKJV in the new testament you see it a lot in the life of the apostles any time the apostles were confronted with a problem, you will read that the and full of the spirit the reacted and it produced the reply to the problem for instance of the Ananias and sapharah issue you see the mantle at work. Peter was just sharp precise and to the point and things happened

Acts 5:1-10

But a certain man named Ananias, with Sapphira his wife, sold a possession,

2 And kept back part of the price, his wife also being privy to it, and brought a certain part, and laid it at the apostles' feet.

3 But Peter said, Ananias, why hath Satan filled thine heart to lie to the Holy Ghost, and to keep back part of the price of the land?

4 Whiles it remained, was it not thine own? and after it was sold, was it not in thine own power? why hast thou conceived this thing in thine heart? thou hast not lied unto men, but unto God.

5 And Ananias hearing these words fell down, and gave up the ghost: and great fear came on all them that heard these things.

6 And the young men arose, wound him up, and carried him out, and buried him.

7 And it was about the space of three hours after, when his wife, not knowing what was done, came in.

8 And Peter answered unto her, Tell me whether ye sold the land for so much? And she said, Yea, for so much.

9 Then Peter said unto her, How is it that ye have agreed together to tempt the Spirit of the Lord? behold, the feet of them which have buried thy husband are at the door, and shall carry thee out.

10 Then fell she down straightway at his feet, and yielded up the ghost: and the young men came in, and found her dead, and, carrying her forth, buried her by her husband.

KJV

Anytime you are operating in your mantle as a servant of God you do not struggle, you just flow. Daniel had a powerful mantle of a prophet and his mantle was very sharp in the area of solving difficult problems Dan 1:17

17 As for these four young men, God gave them knowledge and skill in all literature and wisdom; and Daniel had understanding in all visions and dreams.

NKJV the mantle just makes you know what to do when it comes to problems of its area Dan 5:11-12

11 There is a man in your kingdom in whom is the Spirit of the Holy God. And in the days of your father, light and understanding and wisdom, like the wisdom of the gods, were found in him; and King Nebuchadnezzar your father — your father the king — made him chief of the magicians, astrologers, Chaldeans, and soothsayers. 12 Inasmuch as an excellent spirit, knowledge, understanding, interpreting dreams, solving riddles, and explaining enigmas were found in this Daniel, whom the king named Belteshazzar, now let Daniel be called, and he will give the interpretation."

NKJV

Anytime a man of God ministers and feels as if the anointing wears him or covers him like a cloth, then his mantle has been released. It is up to him to try as much to work hard to make sure it always wears him either by praying for god to keep releasing it and by desiring to stay in the mantle. As he works to let the mantle keep, getting more and more on him the mantle will stay and become a second nature. If the mantle stays, it will begin to stir up other gifts and abilities that are in you and have not been active. The mantle enhances your ministry and gifts to make you effective as a minister.

When ministers say that the fell the presence of God strongly rest upon them in the course of ministration or if even they are not ministering and the feel the stirrings or strong presence that is just upon them then the mantle is reviving or activating itself. In such cases, I recommend that you spend some time enjoying it, making the mantle feel at home, and accepted. Because all the things of God have life force in it, if they are valued they grow, if not given attention they die. It is just like planting a plant, If it not nurtured, watered and cared for it becomes a wild and unpredicted plant and then you lose productivity.

CHAPTER SIX

HINDRANCES TO THE ANOINTING

We must realize that the anointing is God's glory in earthen vessels and the anointed ones are the vessels. We must also recognize that, we determine how much of the anointing will flow through us or how little will flow through us. Primarily we must know that every gift or anointing of God that is released, must have a resting place or else it will lift and go back to heaven. The things of God stay where they are welcome, which means that if you want the anointing to abide in your life, you must create the necessary environment for the anointing to stay upon you and do the work for which it was sent. You must protect the anointing in your life so that you do not miss it or lose it by your carelessness or spiritual theft by others. I have seen people's anointing hijacked by others and used by those who stole it. Moreover, others who's anointing was stolen and could do nothing with their lives. If you value the anointing, you must handle it with care and guard it carefully so that it will not leave you or it will not be stolen or lost. Because you do not get what you, do not treasure.

Lack of peace of mind

The mind is very important in this, because your mind is what communicates with the anointing. You must guard the thoughts that control the mind very carefully. If the mind is not receptive to the anointing it will not listen to anything the anointing is saying, which will make the anointing inactive, because the anointing works through you and with you as you obey his directions. So if you cannot hear it, it will not move. It is therefore important that you tune your mind to listen to the Spirit of and try as much as possible to maintain peace of mind. Because if your mind is distracted you will not flow in the anointing. What the devil will do take away your peace of mind, is to bring the pressures of life upon you. Problems in life, disappointments, failures, betrayals and attacks from people you trusted to disorientate your mind. To protect your mind, you will have to make choices and decisions with protecting the anointing in mind. To hit your mind the devil will use anybody especially people close and dear to you, including your wife so be careful. You must also learn to be immune to attacks on your person, because you will surely have people who are seem to be more religious than you, criticize you. There is no genuinely anointing person whose anointing was not frowned upon before it was accepted do not let doubt take control of your mind, always let your mind be positive and hopeful if possible at all times.

Sadness of heart

Your heart controls your emotions. If you have bright and upbeat emotions, it helps the anointing to flow. I have discovered from experience that the Spirit of God does not live in a sad environment. Joy is a very important part of the anointing. When there is joy, the anointing flows better, so it is important to keep an atmosphere of joy around you. If you have noticed anointing is released when there is worship, and when there is joy in the hearts of the people they can receive. Joy and happiness plays a vital role in the easiness in the flow of anointing, so if you want to flow in the anointing try to be happy and joyful at all times.

Lack of faith

Now he did not do many mighty works there because of their unbelief" Matt. 13:58 Jesus was unable to do much in Nazareth because they did not have faith to receive. if the people you pray for do not expect to receive anything out of your prayer they will receive nothing . Faith plays a vital role for effective working of the anointing. If there is no faith, the anointing will be stifled. As it written in (Heb. 11:6) the anointing is able to achieve great things because of your faith or the faith of the people. Therefore, you must endeavor to create an atmosphere of faith in your life. At times, the devil will attack your faith and if you are not careful, you will lose it. that is why Jude warns us to contend for our faith Jude 3. If you are not careful, you will have faith in the wrong thing. This is equally as dangerous as having no faith. That is why in the letter to the Corinthians, apostle Paul made it clear that he did not want them to believe in scriptural arguments, or stories, or good teaching or personalities like himself and others but in the power of God. 1 Cor.2:4-5. He therefore made it clear that good doctrines or sound biblical teachings were not the prerequisite for God's power, but rather to believe in the sovereign power of God is the key. If you learn to have faith in God, and not teachings, because God is the source of all knowledge, then all things of God will be available. It is very important to have the right foundation for faith or you will believe wrongly and the power will not work. It is not how well you know scripture, then uneducated people will not have access to the anointing. You must believe in your God as Jesus said. (Mark 11:22). Then believe in your self (Mark 11:23), then the people must also believe in what God has given you. (Acts5:11-16). Then things will happen, so it is imperative to feed your soul with faith by learning the Bible and most importantly by listening to stories of faith and inspiration of what God has done in the live of others and testimonies. Because what you do not believe will not happen to you like the official In the days of Elisha 2 kings 7:1-2, and what you do not value you will not enjoy it.

Confused environments

Anointing always comes for specific purposes so it there is no purpose in the environment in which it comes, it will not work. If you take time to study scriptures you will discover that it is only after people's attention had been captured that the anointing moved, everyone the power touched expected to receive something. The anointing never worked, until the attention of the crowd in Jerusalem was upon the apostle Peter. who in the fullness of the anointing preached and souls were convicted Acts 2: 12-14, Acts 2: 37-41. If the people do not believe in your anointing and their mind is occupied with other things then the anointing will not work. Because to receive, you must connect with, tune your mind to the anointing to receive it. It is important that there is no confusion, strife, and contention or the anointing will not have room to operate. if you do not welcome the anointing, and give it your attention, but rather waste your mind on other things like the cares of life, It will die. The parable of the sower taught it clearly Matt13:22. I am not saying do not care about your and responsibilities, but rather manage your time well and have time for the anointing

Sinful lifestyle

I am yet to see a person that God called when he was without sin. The truth is that we all sin and from time to time fall into sin that is why Jesus said to the rich man that (Mark10:18). Everyone is sinful or occasionally we sin against God, that is not what will make you lose the anointing but when you deliberately chose to sin against God. After his warnings, then he will withdraw the power that backs the anointing Until you are empty, like it happened to achan.(Josh. 7:13) so sin can make God turn against you. But at times it is not sin but weights, some people are just weights and are burden some like the hebrews did to Moses (Deut1:37) so the apostle Paul wrote (Heb.12:1-2). There are some weights; you will have to endure, until the Lord removes them. However, do not let it make you lose your cool and make you sin against the Lord. By consistently sinning you give right to the accuser to hinder you anointing, also as you keep sinning a particular sin, the demon behind that kind of sin establishes a covenant with you, which gives it the right to block, steal or hinder your anointing.

Disobedience

The anointing grows with obedience in its use, as you obey the directions it gives you and act on them, you will get the anointing growing stronger. If you refuse to obey, the leading will be stifled and it will not grow into fullness. so disobedience to the leadings of the anointing will hinder it. You will not feel the anointing around you since you are not cooperating. some people are just stubborn doing only what is right in their own eyes and that will always lead you to trouble because there are so many things that you will never know.

Disorder

There must be order in your life and the work. The church must have structures and crusades must be properly organized. Everyone must know his or her place and there must be clear chain of command so that God will know that everyone is not doing what is right in their eyes, but what the servant of God has ordered. If you cannot take orders from the servant of God then the anointing will not flow to you. Like it happened to king saul. 1 sam. 15:22-26 because obedience is a key in the Kingdom. There is order and once the Lord gives the order to his servant he expects everyone under him to follow that directive, and not do what they like. If everybody under the servant of God obeys his orders, the anointing will flow from him through his structure and touch lives. If you do not obey the servant of God, you will be a blockage and a hindrance to the anointing and the life of the people will not be touched effectively, that is why it is important to be of one mind and one heart with the servant of God no matter his faults and weakness. The anointing upon his life must be respected and obeyed. For those under senior ministers you must submit to their authority and supervision or the anointing will not increase or even flow in your life and work.

Fellowship

Fellowship with the Lord is very important, because God is the source of the anointing. as you improve your relationship, he adds more to the anointing till it becomes full, or he quickens the anointing to become sharper and better. If you do not maintain fellowship with the Lord, you hinder the anointing from flowing also. As the Lord visits you in fellowship, any other thing that is a hindrance to the anointing, he will deal with it for the anointing to flow better unhindered.

Prayer

A healthy prayer life is important; if you are not prayerful, you hinder the anointing. It is in the prayer closet that the Lord prepares you to flow in the anointing fully. However, I have also noticed that many prayer warriors do not make real progress in life. I tried to understand why and found out that they believed that they could pray things through and forget their reliance on God. Prayer is nothing without God, if you will believe in God, than on how much or how well you can pray, you will see the anointing grow. You must pray, but you must rely on God not the effectiveness of your prayer. I have a problem with people who glorify prayer, because it is not a replacement for God. If God chooses to answer, it will happen but if he chooses not to answer, nothing will happen, and also if God permits the devil, nothing can make your prayer work. Therefore, you have to pray but you must recognize that if your prayer will work it is at the sovereign will of God. Some people think that God is just principles and formula, but my experience has taught me that God is a sovereign God and he does what pleases him. he can stand on some of those principles to work or he can still chose to work without those principles; or we will not have miracles, which is the temporary setting aside of natural laws for the will and purpose of God to be accomplished. However, yours is to do your best to obey the principles though from time to time, you will find that the Lord in his good pleasure will do what he wants, how he wants it and with whatever reason he wants. so be prayerful to prepare yourself for God to move but as to the moving it is Gods choice.

Curses

When Balaam was invited to curse the Israelites, God moved with every means to prevent Balaam from cursing why ?. once a curse is released it will find a way to work, people like to quote that Prov 26:2

2 Like a flitting sparrow, like a flying swallow,
So a curse without cause shall not alight. NKJV

but people chose to believe one half of that scripture. since a swallow does not stay in the sky but still rests on the ground, a curse that is lunched will finally take effect, because overtime you being a human being will falter and the curse will gain entrance. Every curse depends upon our weakness, every human is weak in one way or another, and the work the anointing set out to do will not be complete. So you must work hard to let the Lord remove curses. In your life always look for trends and patterns in your life that is not right, and ask the Lord to break them. By that, you are purging yourself of every hindrance to the anointing that God has given, every curse in your life gives demons legal rights to work in your life. God who is a respecter of order, will not stop them except in extreme cases or because you have asked for his help. Therefore, watch curses carefully or else you will labor in vain.

Covenants and Spiritual background

Every covenant with demons is a doorway for them to work in your life. If you take items dedicated to demons, you establish covenants with them like achan did with the accursed objectJosh 7:20-26

20 And Achan answered Joshua and said, "Indeed I have sinned against the LORD God of Israel, and this is what I have done: 21 When I saw among the spoils a beautiful Babylonian garment, two hundred shekels of silver, and a wedge of gold weighing fifty shekels, I coveted them and took them. And there they are, hidden in the earth in the midst of my tent, with the silver under it."

22 So Joshua sent messengers, and they ran to the tent; and there it was, hidden in his tent, with the silver under it. 23 And they took them from the midst of the tent, brought them to Joshua and to all the children of Israel, and laid them out before the LORD. 24 Then Joshua, and all Israel with him, took Achan the son of Zerah, the silver, the garment, the wedge of gold, his sons, his daughters, his oxen, his donkeys, his sheep, his tent, and all that he had, and they brought them to the Valley of Achor. 25 And Joshua said,"Why have you troubled us? The LORD will trouble you this day." So all Israel stoned him with stones; and they burned them with fire after they had stoned them with stones.

26 Then they raised over him a great heap of stones, still there to this day. So the LORD turned from the fierceness of His anger. Therefore the name of that place has been called the Valley of Achor to this day.

NKJV. once there is a covenant, God's hand is hindered. The Lord did not move until Gideon destroyed the household gods Judg 6:25-26

25 Now it came to pass the same night that the LORD said to him, "Take your father's young bull, the second bull of seven years old, and tear down the altar of Baal that your father has, and cut down the wooden image that is beside it; 26 and build an altar to the LORD your God on top of this rock in the proper arrangement, and take the second bull and offer a burnt sacrifice with the wood of the image which you shall cut down."

NKJV. It is important to break any past association with demons or else they will come and hinder the anointing. If you have a background in your family line that has covenants with demons, you must work on it and destroy it from your life. it is because of breaking from past covenants, that the Lord asked Abraham to leave his family and kindred so that he can bless him Gen 12:1-2

Now the LORD had said to Abram:

"Get out of your country,
From your family
And from your father's house,
To a land that I will show you.
2 I will make you a great nation;
I will bless you
And make your name great;
And you shall be a blessing.
NKJV . covenants are dangerous, if you form a covenant with a wrong person you will pay dearly1 Kings 20:28-29

28 Then a man of God came and spoke to the king of Israel, and said, "Thus says the LORD: 'Because the Syrians have said, "The LORD is God of the hills, but He is not God of the valleys," therefore I will deliver all this great multitude into your hand, and you shall know that I am the LORD.'"
NKJV
1 Kings 20:31-34

Then his servants said to him, "Look now, we have heard that the kings of the house of Israel are merciful kings. Please, let us put sackcloth around our waists and ropes around our heads, and go out to the king of Israel; perhaps he will spare your life." 32 So they wore sackcloth around their waists and put ropes around their heads, and came to the king of Israel and said, "Your servant Ben-Hadad says, 'Please let me live.'"

And he said, "Is he still alive? He is my brother."

33 Now the men were watching closely to see whether any sign of mercy would come from him; and they quickly grasped at this word and said, "Your brother Ben-Hadad."

So he said, "Go, bring him." Then Ben-Hadad came out to him; and he had him come up into the chariot.

34 So Ben-Hadad said to him,"The cities which my father took from your father I will restore; and you may set up marketplaces for yourself in Damascus, as my father did in Samaria."

Then Ahab said, "I will send you away with this treaty." So he made a treaty with him and sent him away.
NKJV these pieces of scripture illustrate the fact that people take advantage of our kindlnes to get us into agreements and covenants that are detrimental to us because of that covenant that ahab did he lost a great opportunity and got punished1 Kings 20:39-42
9 Now as the king passed by, he cried out to the king and said, "Your servant went out into the midst of the battle; and there, a man came over and brought a man to me, and said, 'Guard this man; if by any means he is missing, your life shall be for his life, or else you shall pay a talent of silver.' 40 While your servant was busy here and there, he was gone."

Then the king of Israel said to him, "So shall your judgment be; you yourself have decided it."

41 And he hastened to take the bandage away from his eyes; and the king of Israel recognized him as one of the prophets. 42 Then he said to him, "Thus says the LORD:'Because you have let slip out of your hand a man whom I appointed to utter destruction, therefore your life shall go for his life, and your people for his people.'"
NKJV From my experience as a minister of God, I have observed that many of the problems many people have are from their marriage. it is either that the other partner is demonized or coming from a heavily demonic

background, so it becomes a door of entry and demons will use it to hinder the anointing. I know of cases of pastors who have wives involved in witchcraft and as a result if which they are not making progress in life and ministry. So be careful about covenants and Spiritual backgrounds especially people with strange demonic background. Be sure of your spouse and friends that they do not have covenants that will work against you.

CHAPTER SEVEN
HUMAN DIMENSION OF THE ANOINTING

The human nature of the man of God is his weakness and also his strength. Every attack of Satan and his agents is to influence the human nature. You need depth of character, will and inner strength of mind to make sure you do see the end of your work. I have known men and women who had incredible gifts and powerful anointing and did not achieve anything with it because of a human weakness or inability to manipulate human nature to achieve with the anointing. For every anointing to go far, and achieve more, human nature must be on your side supporting you. Jesus could not do much in his home town because his people did not accept his ministry. And it was the testimony of the Samaritan woman that gave Jesus the breakthrough in Samaria. No matter how much a thing is of God, if humans do not accept it, it will not work because God does not violate freewill, he gives us the power of choice. The devil having studied human nature over time has mastered how to manipulate human nature to his ends. So we must understand that the human side of the anointing is the make or break for every anointing. mental development is a major factor in achieving with the anointing, that is why the Bible tells us that wisdom is the principal thing and also that it is important to renew our mind. The broadness and depth of your mind, foresight and intelligence will guarantee your success. The reason three thousand souls believed on the day of Pentecost was attributed to the human nature of curiosity apart from the anointing of the Spirit at work. It was strange to them, the things the believers did, like speaking in tongues and foreign language, which is what, got the attention of the people. The reason the governor believed Paul was not the gospel he preached but the blinding of Elymas the sorcerer, which was spectacular. The reason the Samaritan believed Jesus was, he told her the secrets of her life and Nathaniel believed because Jesus told him where he was standing before he came and his heart. Lack of good organization has denied many anointed ministers the structure and the platform to excel. Since they might not be enlightened mentally, they do not understand what they do well and so they accept little as their portion in God, whereas they could have gone very far. There are certain kinds of people who can take your ministry far, people of substance, worth, dedicated, loyal, influential people, intelligent and brilliant people etc and if you do not realize it, discover, and bring them to you, you will struggle in the ministry. If there were not educated men like Paul, much of what we call Christian doctrine would have been lost. it is paramount to improve yourself as a human being, In fact that is the essence of the law and the prophets. So that you can go far with what God had given you. In the parable of the talents, the master gave each according to his abilities and then they used their abilities to manage and in the end it showed. if you improve your abilities, your anointing will achieve more; so the size of your anointing is not as important as the size of your abilities, which is the key. Over time, I have observed that the kind of spiritual nature and motivation an anointed person has, determines how far their anointing will go. The determination and sacrifice of these anointed ones is the cause of how far they went. Elijah wanted to turn the hearts of Israel back to God so he went into prayer and took a bold step and he became a great man. Elisha though he carried double the anointing of Elijah could not set his own pace he lived under the shadow of Elijah. Some might argue that the anointing he had was from Elijah so he could do no further but you will admit that Joshua received the anointing of Moses but he also set his own records he also did something remarkable, he made the sun and the moon stand and no one has been able to do that. One thing I noticed about pacesetters in the anointing was that they had a dream, a hope, an ideal they were looking for" Heb 11:1

Now faith is the substance of things hoped for, the evidence
NKJVHeb 11:14-16
14 For those who say such things declare plainly that they seek a homeland.
15 And truly if they had called to mind that country from which they had come out, they would have had opportunity to return.

NKJV, they worked, suffered, sacrificed. In fact paid the price for the anointing to be released but most of those who inherited their anointing did not catch the vision of the original owner and made no effort or little effort to grasp the vision for which the power of the anointing was released so it became lost over time and the anointing lost their significance. The battles of Christendom would have been much reduced if those who inherited powerful anointing had passed it on and those who received it had seen the significance and used it too. The anointing of Elijah had been to spiritually oversee and watch over Israel as a nation, judge people that were doing evil and were building doors for demons to enter Israel. However, since Elisha did not realize the importance of passing it on, it went to the grave with him. That is why Elisha could see anything that happened in Israel as the Lord wanted and could always get a solution to their problems. We need to understand that anointing while given is the sole responsibility of the recipient, and he has every right to use it as he deems fit. He can help it grow and increase or die, because every thing of God is living and they grow only by use and practice, that is why apostle Paul wrote concerning growing in the Spirit of the word of God Heb 5:14

4 But solid food belongs to those who are of full age, that is, those who by reason of use have their senses exercised to discern both good and evil.

NKJV. as you exert the anointing you begin to understand its methods of operations, limits and abilities, as you grow in use the anointing grows. I have observed people and have learnt that the ones that use their anointing more become stronger, and people are not able to make use of their anointing because they did not experiment with it, and grow to master the use so it died or the growth was hindered or subdued. From time to time you meet ministers who are very anointed of God but are making little impact, and get people with little anointing and making more impact. I sought to find a reason for It and I found that the level of mental enlightenment was a major factor. Those with broader minds and more knowledge made more impact and the illiterate ones made very little impact through more anointed. If you study the new testament we see that the unschooled apostles like Peter were very anointed but the educated one's like Paul left us more material than all the other apostles combined. Peter admitted Paul 's level of mental development. 2 Peter 3:15-16

15 and consider that the longsuffering of our Lord is salvation — as also our beloved brother Paul, according to the wisdom given to him, has written to you, 16 as also in all his epistles, speaking in them of these

things, in which are some things hard to understand, which untaught and unstable people twist to their own destruction, as they do also the rest of the Scriptures.

NKJV and Paul also recognized that these apostles were more anointed than him1 Cor 15:9-10

9 For I am the least of the apostles, who am not worthy to be called an apostle, because I persecuted the church of God. 10 But by the grace of God I am what I am, and His grace toward me was not in vain; but I labored more abundantly than they all, yet not I, but the grace of God which was with me.

NKJV . but yet he accomplished more than them. If you consider the high point of Peter's healing ministry, he did not even touch people Acts 5:15-16

15 so that they brought the sick out into the streets and laid them on beds and couches, that at least the shadow of Peter passing by might fall on some of them. 16 Also a multitude gathered from the surrounding cities to Jerusalem, bringing sick people and those who were tormented by unclean spirits, and they were all healed.

NKJV and the high point of the healing ministry of Paul where there still had to be transferred through touch Acts 19:11-12

Now God worked unusual miracles by the hands of Paul, 12 so that even handkerchiefs or aprons were brought from his body to the sick, and the diseases left them and the evil spirits went out of them.

NKJV . you will realize the difference but he accomplished more because he was better enlightened and mentally trained. That is why it is important to study and broaden the scope of our knowledge 2 Tim 2:15-16

15 Be diligent to present yourself approved to God, a worker who does not need to be ashamed, rightly dividing the word of truth.

NKJV. I was discussing the state of Christian thought ,and I was lamenting that the Christian faith has lacked thinkers and philosophers who could help us understand the practicality of the gospel better, and now what we get are messages by pastors which are just copies or rather rearrangements of scriptures or other peoples messages and so we have lost touch with the reality of the gospel in a lot of areas of our lives. While the secular world and other religions are busy expanding and developing their philosophies, the church has gone to sleep and lost touch with the greatest philosopher the Lord God almighty, the source of wisdom, the creator. Instead of being the people other religions look to now we are looking to other religions and the secular world. In Africa I know of pastors and Christians who go to fetish priests for protection and help to prosper and this has been the source of divining Spirits in the prophetic ministries in Africa. I was talking to a man who was telling me that, if God does not start moving in the life of his people a lot of people will fall away and I felt he was right. If you listen to a lot of ministers, what they preach is neither relevant or now it is mostly motivational messages and pure condemnation of certain practices that they deem wrong. But what most preachers do not realize is that the preaching of the gospel was a demonstration of power 1 Cor 2:4-5

4 And my speech and my preaching were not with persuasive words of human wisdom, but in demonstration of the Spirit and of power, 5 that your faith should not be in the wisdom of men but in the power of God. NKJV , Heb 2:3-4

4 God also bearing witness both with signs and wonders, with various miracles, and gifts of the Holy Spirit, according to His own will? NKJV. these days you go to church to hear human philosophies backed with scripture quotations, or for the other side of balance we are told to stay away from certain sins that if we live righteous lives, God will bless us. I am not condemning anybody or what they do but I am pleading with all that let us bring the living power of God back into the Gospel. God will still from time to time do something to keep the hope of his people alive but we have not entered the real thing. People still feel empty and find solace in trying other things like new age religions, etc because we do not have answers to their problems. It is only when they have a spiritual encounter with God, that they become believers. I tell people that when a preacher is preaching and saying that if you live a holy life God will bless you, I laugh because it takes more than a holy life for God to bless. Jesus said it " except your righteousness exceeds that of the Pharisees and Sadducees, you cannot enter the Kingdom" it takes an encounter with God to be blessed, it is time we begin to realize that God is the main thing, he is the solution to our every problem and Jesus died and rose to make a way to God. These days another doctrine is sublimely creeping into the church of God that Jesus is God, which is false, Jesus is the son of God plain and simple. we are making Jesus God and leaving God out of our lives gradually but how can we breathe without air. That is what we are doing with our maker; you may survive a little but will eventually die. Who we are will determine how far our anointing will go. If we develop ourselves, we will go further with the anointing we have received" 2 Tim 2:20-21

20 But in a great house there are not only vessels of gold and silver, but also of wood and clay, some for honor and some for dishonor. 21 Therefore if anyone cleanses himself from the latter, he will be a vessel for honor, sanctified and useful for the Master, prepared for every good work. NKJV you level of self-preparation ad development will determine how far you will go with the anointing.

Your physique is very important in your ability to handle the anointing, if you are not physically strong you cannot carry heavy anointing. if you ask anyone who has encountered the anointing or the presence of God he or she will tell you that the anointing weakens you physically if it is not released but if it is being released you are very strong. The anointing uses your body to do its work through you so it takes a toll on your strength. So if you do not learn to rest periodically or take time to relax after a heavy burst of anointing, you will get a breakdown someday in your health. When the anointing finishes using your body, it will leave so you must replenish the lost energy. since the anointing uses your strength, you must exercise, eat well and be fit so that you can always be useful for the anointing of God. another human area of the anointing is stress. The anointing is a spiritual thing, and it communicates with the body through the mind. At times, we stress ourselves trying to get into the anointing or our problems can put us under so much stress that we lose touch with the spiritual. Therefore, we do not connect entirely with the anointing or in our self doubt we do not yield ourselves fully to the Spirit of God. At times, we are so distracted and stressed up by the problems of life that the anointing does not flow through us. It is really important to make sure we keep stress levels down, the anointing of God flows and works in relaxed environments especially joyful ones. You also need to have a personal revelation of God. It is upon that revelation that you will be able to walk in the fullness of the anointing. Most of the time most ministers live upon other peoples revelations of God. Therefore, their anointing is not fully effective because the anointing flows with you based upon certain level of revelations of God in your life. if you do not grow in your relationship with God in your level of understanding in God then your anointing will stop growing. This brings me to a key much talked about area, mentoring. From my experience and observation of ministers and lives of Christians and as I sought the face to the Lord on it I learned something, some people must be mentored by men and some must be mentored by God. some people can make their own ways but the ways of some is chosen for them by God. ("Ps 37:23

23 The steps of a good man are ordered by the LORD,
And He delights in his way.
NKJV , Prov 16:2

2 All the ways of a man are pure in his own eyes,
But the LORD weighs the spirits.
NKJV for most people you need one mentor. but in the case of people with special assignments for God, he or she must go through paths that the Lord has chosen so that he can teach him the lessons that he wants to teach them Certain things that are critical to the success of their assignments that the Lord has for them. most people will need one mentor all their life but some will need several mentors and even some will need non but the last is very rare. Like Elijah, Moses, Abraham. Such people are on pacesetting assignments and they are bringing new wine so it is important in the eyes of God that we do not put new wine in old wineskins, which is old perceptions and teachings which will not be relevant to us in that new move of God. as apostle Paul wrote" Heb 1:1

God, who at various times and in various ways spoke in time past to the fathers by the prophets,
NKJ I believe the church is still growing in revelation and understanding of God and the things of God. for instance, in times past it was thought that Christians are poor, now the revelation of prosperity has come to stay; who knows what other things that we think are right but are wrong about God . but most people will have to be mentored and guided by men who are on the work but for a select few they are to take over from what the one ahead of him has done like Elijah and Elisha, Moses and Joshua. Such people grow to become exactly a copy of their mentor and when the time is up for the old man to go, his mantle is passed on to the mentored to keep the fire in the next generation. And in some cases anointing shifts from one to another but God does not want the recipient to make a mistake that the former made so in such cases he sends him around different places to learn from others before he directs him to the exact person he wants to hand over to him the mantle. One thing I also learnt is that when two people are called to different visions, they will not agree and will not be able to work on one vision except they are matured. But it will still not be

for long because their assignments are different that is why some people cannot work under anyone because they are called to be head so they cannot be under someone for long but do not confuse greed and selfishness which motivates some people but rather I am talking of genuinely anointed people. And if a person with a bigger anointing is under one with a smaller anointing there will be friction until each anointing finds its place or one leaves the other and order is in place. In such cases it might be that a younger minister carrying the bigger anointing and then because of his age the older folks do not want to lead but God chooses what he likes not what man likes. Another thing you must understand about the anointing is that it is God's property and it uses you and not you using it. At times there is the danger of the anointing being abused. The anointing at times sanctions what a man of God says, despite that at that moment it is no the will of God but that of the servant.Isa 44:26

26 Who confirms the word of His servant,

And performs the counsel of His messengers;

Who says to Jerusalem, 'You shall be inhabited,'

To the cities of Judah, 'You shall be built,'

And I will raise up her waste places;

NKJV) that is why God must trust you to give his power to you most times God holds the servant responsible for his choices. what happens is that as the anointing begins to work, People start to recognize you and if you are not careful out of genuine desire to help people you will stretch the anointing to where it does not and will not go. In such cases the anointing will not work so there is a vacuum, which the devil will fill. That is how genuine man or woman of God became false prophets, because the devil starts to show them visions and back him up with power so he or she feels that the Lord is with him. In my opinion, it is the best trap of the devil has been setting for men of God and they falling a lot into it. There are levels of anointing that the Lord gives and he increases it in his own time and in his own will but in our desire to become more powerful some start to seek mere power and the devil fills the void. I know a lot of men and women of God the Lord has told me have fallen into that trap and once the devil walks in, God walks out and it is difficult if not impossible to convince such people that the Lord has left them because they are living right and the power is still moving in their life. One thing I have learnt from the Lord is that the source of the power backing whatever you say or do is the main thing. These days the devil has got so smarter, so it is not just by their fruits, ye shall know them because their lifestyle can be clean but at the end of their ministry. It will speak for itself it is very important for us all to always be on your guard for slight changes and be sure the devil is not gradually creeping into your anointing just as he tried to play simple harmless looking tricks upon Jesus. In some case a person might be young but anointed by God because God does what pleases him. In such cases my advice to such a fellow is to be careful of your fellow ministers especially of their envy and jealousy, at the same time make it a point to be humble to seek divine counsel and the counsel of mature men with caution. Because if you remember it was the old prophet who deceived the anointed young prophet to disobey the Lord. One of the biggest problems that young anointed people face is persecution because of their age, but it is part of your cross and my advice is to depend more on the Lord and try to keep your mouth shut so that the elders do not envy you and plot your downfall. Human beings are human beings so always be on the lookout for the base nature of man in yourself and in others so that your anointing does not get cut off along the way. It was the people that made Moses disobey the Lord so be careful. Most persecution that anointed people face is based on envy and jealousies of other people towards them. Examples are Jesus and the Jewish elders, Daniel and his fellow ministers, David and Saul, Joseph and his brothers, human nature is a very dangerous thing. So if you want to succeed as an anointed person then watch how you deal with your fellow human beings not to cause strife and jealousy also people find it difficult to get their ego bruised. If you hurt the ego or pride of a person of influence or power, he will bring you down. It has affected great ministers so do not fall for it even your workers can plot some evil for you out of envy or bruised ego or because you hurt them and they want revenge. God will lift you up but why let yourself fall and then struggle to rise again. Though the Bible asks Christians not to give space for such things, I am bringing you to reality, from time to time, human nature will rear its head so as you deal with people never underestimate the human nature in those individuals and handle them carefully. Also the more people know you, the more familiar they become with you and if you do not guard against it you will lost respect and the anointing will lose its honor. You must protect the dignity of the anointing and lookout for opportunities to let those around you respect you. When you have a good report people find it easy to accept you. I am not saying you would have to please people but rather be a principled person so that you will be someone people will look up to when they need divine counsel and godly

advice. we all have issues in our life, but we must be careful that it does not become a stumbling block to our anointing reaching the people.
Self discipline and self control is very important "1 Cor 9:24-27

Do you not know that those who run in a race all run, but one receives the prize? Run in such a way that you may obtain it. 25 And everyone who competes for the prize is temperate in all things. Now they do it to obtain a perishable crown, but we for an imperishable crown. 26 Therefore I run thus: not with uncertainty. Thus I fight: not as one who beats the air. 27 But I discipline my body and bring it into subjection, lest, when I have preached to others, I myself should become disqualified.
NKJV you have to constantly be on the lookout on your life. If not, you will gradually slip in your standards in life, in areas that you consider insignificant but very critical for your success as an anointed person. The ones that must be careful are those that are on higher levels. If you do not watch yourself well, you will set yourself up for downfall. So you must always keep your life in check and make sure that you do not go out of control. If you get absolute, you will be easily corrupted and destroyed. So be constantly watchful on all areas of your life. I always say that there is a fine line between sin and holiness so if you are not watchful before you realize, you are down so be watchful and keep your life in check.
Another area to watch is making sure people do not hold grudges against you. If you are not careful it will hinder you, that is why the Bible says" (Heb 12:14

14 Pursue peace with all people, and holiness, without which no one will see the Lord:
NKJv), and the Lord Jesus said "John 20:23
23 If you forgive the sins of any, they are forgiven them; if you retain the sins of any, they are retained."
NKJV and he even made it clearer" Matt 5:23-26
23 Therefore if you bring your gift to the altar, and there remember that your brother has something against you, 24 leave your gift there before the altar, and go your way. First be reconciled to your brother, and then come and offer your gift. 25 Agree with your adversary quickly, while you are on the way with him, lest your adversary deliver you to the judge, the judge hand you over to the officer, and you be thrown into prison. 26 Assuredly, I say to you, you will by no means get out of there till you have paid the last penny.

NKJV so be careful of human holds. If humans hold it against you, they will be a blockage to your blessing. It is not that God has not blessed you or anointed you but rather every hold is blocking you. until it is settled, you will not be able to physically enjoy what God has given you. A most important area of the anointing is your human relationships. How you build relationships. The person close to you can drain you or fill you up, if you are in the midst of wrong person they will spoil your day. If problematic people they will drain you emotionally like happened to Moses as a result of which in his outburst he disobeyed God (Num 20:2-12

2 Now there was no water for the congregation; so they gathered together against Moses and Aaron. 3 And the people contended with Moses and spoke, saying: "If only we had died when our brethren died before the LORD! 4 Why have you brought up the assembly of the LORD into this wilderness, that we and our animals should die here? 5 And why have you made us come up out of Egypt, to bring us to this evil place? It is not a place of grain or figs or vines or pomegranates; nor is there any water to drink." 6 So Moses and Aaron went from the presence of the assembly to the door of the tabernacle of meeting, and they fell on their faces. And the glory of the LORD appeared to them.

7 Then the LORD spoke to Moses, saying, 8 "Take the rod; you and your brother Aaron gather the congregation together. Speak to the rock before their eyes, and it will yield its water; thus you shall bring water for them out of the rock, and give drink to the congregation and their animals." 9 So Moses took the rod from before the LORD as He commanded him.

10 And Moses and Aaron gathered the assembly together before the rock; and he said to them,"Hear now, you rebels! Must we bring water for you out of this rock?" 11 Then Moses lifted his hand and struck the rock twice with his rod; and water came out abundantly, and the congregation and their animals drank.

12 Then the LORD spoke to Moses and Aaron, "Because you did not believe Me, to hallow Me in the eyes of the children of Israel, therefore you shall not bring this assembly into the land which I have given them." NKJV Eli's relationship with his children caused his downfall because he did not discipline them.(1 Sam 2:22-36

Now Eli was very old; and he heard everything his sons did to all Israel, and how they lay with the women who assembled at the door of the tabernacle of meeting. 23 So he said to them, "Why do you do such things? For I hear of your evil dealings from all the people. 24 No, my sons! For it is not a good report that I hear. You make the LORD's people transgress. 25 If one man sins against another, God will judge him. But if a man sins against the LORD, who will intercede for him?" Nevertheless they did not heed the voice of their father, because the LORD desired to kill them.

26 And the child Samuel grew in stature, and in favor both with the LORD and men.

27 Then a man of God came to Eli and said to him, "Thus says the LORD:'Did I not clearly reveal Myself to the house of your father when they were in Egypt in Pharaoh's house? 28 Did I not choose him out of all the tribes of Israel to be My priest, to offer upon My altar, to burn incense, and to wear an ephod before Me? And did I not give to the house of your father all the offerings of the children of Israel made by fire? 29 Why do you kick at My sacrifice and My offering which I have commanded in My dwelling place, and honor your sons more than Me, to make yourselves fat with the best of all the offerings of Israel My people?' 30 Therefore the LORD God of Israel says:'I said indeed that your house and the house of your father would walk before Me forever.' But now the LORD says:'Far be it from Me; for those who honor Me I will honor, and those who despise Me shall be lightly esteemed. 31 Behold, the days are coming that I will cut off your arm and the arm of your father's house, so that there will not be an old man in your house. 32 And you will see an enemy in My dwelling place, despite all the good which God does for Israel. And there shall not be an old man in your house forever. 33 But any of your men whom I do not cut off from My altar shall consume your eyes and grieve your heart. And all the descendants of your house shall die in the flower of their age. 34 Now this shall be a sign to you that will come upon your two sons, on Hophni and Phinehas: in one day they shall die, both of them. 35 Then I will raise up for Myself a faithful priest who shall do according to what is in My heart and in My mind. I will build him a sure house, and he shall walk before My anointed forever. 36 And it shall come to pass that everyone who is left in your house will come and bow down to him for a piece of silver and a morsel of bread, and say, "Please, put me in one of the priestly positions, that I may eat a piece of bread.""

NKJV It is therefore important to discipline your children. In addition, the wives of Solomon turned him away from the Lord 1 Kings 11:1-11

But King Solomon loved many foreign women, as well as the daughter of Pharaoh: women of the Moabites, Ammonites, Edomites, Sidonians, and Hittites — 2 from the nations of whom the LORD had said to the children of Israel,"You shall not intermarry with them, nor they with you. Surely they will turn away your hearts after their gods." Solomon clung to these in love. 3 And he had seven hundred wives, princesses, and three hundred concubines; and his wives turned away his heart. 4 For it was so, when Solomon was old, that his wives turned his heart after other gods; and his heart was not loyal to the LORD his God, as was the heart of his father David. 5 For Solomon went after Ashtoreth the goddess of the Sidonians, and after Milcom the abomination of the Ammonites. 6 Solomon did evil in the sight of the LORD, and did not fully follow the LORD, as did his father David. 7 Then Solomon built a high place for Chemosh the abomination of Moab, on the hill that is east of Jerusalem, and for Molech the abomination of the people of Ammon. 8 And he did likewise for all his foreign wives, who burned incense and sacrificed to their gods.

9 So the LORD became angry with Solomon, because his heart had turned from the LORD God of Israel, who had appeared to him twice, 10 and had commanded him concerning this thing, that he should not go after other gods; but he did not keep what the LORD had commanded. 11 Therefore the LORD said to Solomon, "Because you have done this, and have not kept My covenant and My statutes, which I have commanded you, I will surely tear the kingdom away from you and give it to your servant.
NKJV Samson's girlfriend Delilah sold him to his enemies and destroyed the secret of his strength (Judg 16:4-21

4 Afterward it happened that he loved a woman in the Valley of Sorek, whose name was Delilah. 5 And the lords of the Philistines came up to her and said to her,"Entice him, and find out where his great strength lies, and by what means we may overpower him, that we may bind him to afflict him; and every one of us will give you eleven hundred pieces of silver."
6 So Delilah said to Samson, "Please tell me where your great strength lies, and with what you may be bound to afflict you."
7 And Samson said to her, "If they bind me with seven fresh bowstrings, not yet dried, then I shall become weak, and be like any other man."

8 So the lords of the Philistines brought up to her seven fresh bowstrings, not yet dried, and she bound him with them. 9 Now men were lying in wait, staying with her in the room. And she said to him, "The Philistines are upon you, Samson!" But he broke the bowstrings as a strand of yarn breaks when it touches fire. So the secret of his strength was not known.

10 Then Delilah said to Samson, "Look, you have mocked me and told me lies. Now, please tell me what you may be bound with."

11 So he said to her, "If they bind me securely with new ropes that have never been used, then I shall become weak, and be like any other man."

12 Therefore Delilah took new ropes and bound him with them, and said to him, "The Philistines are upon you, Samson!" And men were lying in wait, staying in the room. But he broke them off his arms like a thread.

13 Delilah said to Samson, "Until now you have mocked me and told me lies. Tell me what you may be bound with."

And he said to her, "If you weave the seven locks of my head into the web of the loom" —

14 So she wove it tightly with the batten of the loom, and said to him, "The Philistines are upon you, Samson!" But he awoke from his sleep, and pulled out the batten and the web from the loom.

15 Then she said to him,"How can you say, 'I love you,' when your heart is not with me? You have mocked me these three times, and have not told me where your great strength lies." 16 And it came to pass, when she pestered him daily with her words and pressed him, so that his soul was vexed to death, 17 that he told her all his heart, and said to her,"No razor has ever come upon my head, for I have been a Nazirite to God from my mother's womb. If I am shaven, then my strength will leave me, and I shall become weak, and be like any other man."

18 When Delilah saw that he had told her all his heart, she sent and called for the lords of the Philistines, saying, "Come up once more, for he has told me all his heart." So the lords of the Philistines came up to her and brought the money in their hand. 19 Then she lulled him to sleep on her knees, and called for a man and had him shave off the seven locks of his head. Then she began to torment him, and his strength left him. 20 And she said, "The Philistines are upon you, Samson!" So he awoke from his sleep, and said, "I will go out as before, at other times, and shake myself free!" But he did not know that the LORD had departed from him.

21 Then the Philistines took him and put out his eyes, and brought him down to Gaza. They bound him with bronze fetters, and he became a grinder in the prison.

NKJV, so watch the people you build relationship with and how you treat them they can bring your downfall. So many men of God did not last because their wives turned their hearts away or frustrated them from the work of God. So watch yourself, and how you build your relationships. Jesus chose rich people as friends and he chose hardworking people not lazy people as his disciples. Therefore, his ministry was successful; it is up to you but choose wisely. If you are well connected to influential and resourceful and people you will go far or else. If you choose the wrong crowd, you will fail. Prov 27:17

17 As iron sharpens iron,
So a man sharpens the countenance of his friend.
NKJV; Prov 24:6
6 For by wise counsel you will wage your own war,
And in a multitude of counselors there is safety.
NKJV
If you walk with people of positive influence, people will accept you. Acceptance is a critical key to your anointing making a mark; Jesus could not do miracles because the people did not accept him in Nazareth. acceptance is very necessary for your anointing to excel Matt 13:54-58
54 When He had come to His own country, He taught them in their synagogue, so that they were astonished and said, "Where did this Man get this wisdom and these mighty works? 55 Is this not the carpenter's son? Is not His mother called Mary? And His brothers James, Joses, Simon, and Judas? 56 And His sisters, are they not all with us? Where then did this Man get all these things?" 57 So they were offended at Him.

But Jesus said to them, "A prophet is not without honor except in his own country and in his own house." 58 Now He did not do many mighty works there because of their unbelief.
NKJv so if people know you too well, your weakness and strength, your effectiveness is compromised that is why Jesus did not give himself to men. When people get familiar with you, they despise or do not believe the anointing. So guard your anointing from all these negative human influences on the anointing and use it to rather grow the anointing to greatness.
Watch out for pride, if you are proud it can set you up for a fall; you must learn to handle issues with maturity not pride or else people will resent and not cooperate with their spirit. Since you need the cooperation of the

people to release the anointing into their lives for results, if you are full of pride they will not like to see your face or they will not cooperate in their spirit with you and they will not celebrate you. As this happens gradually, people leave or start to slander you. You must understand that not matter how Spirit filled we are, we are human so all these human fruits that scripture admonish us against will always rear their head and our duty is constantly keep it in check and control it, fits of anger can gradually drive the people you hurt away from you and gradually isolate you. This will give the devil the chance to destroy you, so you must understand that you need people to push you up. Every Spiritual gift must be seen in operation physically and people will have to yield themselves for you to release your gift to operate on them so do not be proud, if the people are not there, you are not there. it is our duty to let the Lord help us as anointed people to change our life to be the partakers of divine nature but the people you preach to are sinners and new believer and not mature people so the human weakness is there so we must handle with care as God works on them.

One thing that can destroy anointing is misinterpretation, how people interpret, what you say and do is very important, your actions and words must be interpreted in good terms or else people will isolate and reject you. Make sure your actions and words are rightly understood, and clear for your success to be sure.

There is an element of unpredictability and yet reliability with the gifts of God. Each gift and anointing is tailored or created with an individual personality in mind, your character can color your anointing. If you are bold by nature, your anointing thrives with boldness; if you are lazy it becomes lazy. In fact, the anointing changes your character but your personality also changes your anointing, so there is a gradual blending of the two until oneness is achieved. if you have a character trait it will affect your anointing negatively and if you have a good character trait it will affect your anointing positively so you must watch your character. The uniqueness of every gift however similar is the humanity of the anointed and his weakness and strength, personality and style are important parts of the anointing, if all these humanity, mistakes are lost then the gift will no more be special and effective. It will lose its colorfulness' and become dull, from my walk in the Lord, I have learnt there is no spiritual thing that is not manifested physically. Moreover, if it will happen physically, it will take serious committed sacrificial work to bring it to pass so if you let people treat anyhow they will not put in the seriousness required to make it happen. Any anointing that is not making physical impact is not yet complete, it takes the acceptance of the people for the anointing of God to work in their lives. So the anointing of God is tailored to meet the needs of the people, even if it is the will of God it will be tailored to meet the people's need. If you do not win the heart of people, your anointing will not be seen. If you do not meet the needs of the people, you will not be relevant and they will not come to you. It does not mean you must compromise the principles of God but rather you must position yourself such that you become relevant to the people. In such a case, the anointing will flow mightily because the people are hungry for what you have and you will be used of God. Remember that though God anointed David king, it took the people to be willing to accept and make him king before he became king.

Make no mistake, you can be anointed and fail. The anointing is a special gift of God but you are responsible for how you use it. There are quite a few reasons why it does happen. Most of us never get to use our anointing fully all our life. We also abuse and misuse the anointing and its privileges for example, Solomon was anointed with wisdom and had the privilege of sitting on the throne of his father, and he started to follow strange women and he did not finish as great as he could have. 1 Kings 11:1-4

But King Solomon loved many foreign women , as well as the daughter of Pharaoh: women of the Moabites, Ammonites, Edomites, Sidonians, and Hittites — 2 from the nations of whom the LORD had said to the children of Israel,"You shall not intermarry with them, nor they with you. Surely they will turn away your hearts after their gods." Solomon clung to these in love. 3 And he had seven hundred wives, princesses, and three hundred concubines; and his wives turned away his heart. 4 For it was so, when Solomon was old, that his wives turned his heart after other gods; and his heart was not loyal to the LORD his God, as was the heart of his father David.

NKJV

Gideon was given the privilege to be the judge of the whole Israel and he refused the opportunity and rather set the stage for Israel to worship idol. Judg 8:22-25

Then the men of Israel said to Gideon ,"Rule over us, both you and your son, and your grandson also; for you have delivered us from the hand of Midian."

23 But Gideon said to them, "I will not rule over you, nor shall my son rule over you; the LORD shall rule over you." 24 Then Gideon said to them, "I would like to make a request of you, that each of you would give me the earrings from his plunder." For they had golden earrings, because they were Ishmaelites.

25 So they answered, "We will gladly give them." And they spread out a garment, and each man threw into it the earrings from his plunder.
NKJV.......Judg 8:27
27 Then Gideon made it into an ephod and set it up in his city, Ophrah. And all Israel played the harlot with it there. It became a snare to Gideon and to his house.
NKJV

And there are many other examples of men and women of God. A lot of people rely on the anointing as a refuge and think that the anointing will deal with all their problems, but you must do what is your part. Samuel was a great man of God but he failed as a father, because of which the privilege of being the judge of isreal was taken from him and the people chose a king 1 Sam 8:1-5

Now it came to pass when Samuel was old that he made his sons judges over Israel. 2 The name of his firstborn was Joel, and the name of his second, Abijah; they were judges in Beersheba. 3 But his sons did not walk in his ways; they turned aside after dishonest gain, took bribes, and perverted justice.

4 Then all the elders of Israel gathered together and came to Samuel at Ramah, 5 and said to him, "Look, you are old, and your sons do not walk in your ways. Now make us a king to judge us like all the nations."
NKJV
David was also a failure as a father yet a great king, where he should have disciplined his son ammon for committing incest he was angry but did nothing about it. He seemed to be ineffective in calling his sons to order such that Absalom crowned himself king without any fear of his father. Adonijah also did the same thing even when his father had not named him and his father was not dead, they seemed to show him not respect as the father, maybe that is why he might have chosen Solomon to be in his place.
At times fear can also have us not act in the authorithy God has given us by the anointing, it nearly happened to apostle peter twice. First before he

went to preach to cornelus when God had sent him to go to the gentile he was afraid of the rection of his fellow jews. It took a rebuke from the lord to get peter to go to the house of cornelus which opened a new chapter for the Christian faith and the work of God. Even after obeying the Lord he still had to explain himself and defend that it was the Lord that instructed him to the whole church to avoid being condemned. Secondly he had out of fear stopped eating with Gentile Christians when the Jewish Christians came from Jerusalem to visit him, which made apostle Paul rebuke him in front of all. Gal 2:11-14

Now when Peter had come to Antioch, I withstood him to his face, because he was to be blamed; 12 for before certain men came from James, he would eat with the Gentiles; but when they came, he withdrew and separated himself, fearing those who were of the circumcision. 13 And the rest of the Jews also played the hypocrite with him, so that even Barnabas was carried away with their hypocrisy.

14 But when I saw that they were not straightforward about the truth of the gospel, I said to Peter before them all,"If you, being a Jew, live in the manner of Gentiles and not as the Jews, why do you compel Gentiles to live as Jews?
NKJV
Sometimes we can become covetous and greedy for example king saul disobeyed direct instructions from the lord to destroy all he saw in the land of amalek but rather he chose to save the lives of the livestock of the people and the king and queen. Sometimes it could be because of pity that some did not go as far as they should in destroying evil. Whatever the reasons for limiting the anointing we should try to take the limits of and go the whole distance.

Seasons of the anointing

Every anointing has life because it is from God, and everything that comes from God is living and has a life of its own to accomplish what it was sent to do. Therefore, there is a process of bonding that must go on, between the recipient of the anointing and the anointing. The anointing teaches the recipient until it bonds to become one with the recipient.
1 John 2:27

27 But the anointing which you have received from Him abides in you, and you do not need that anyone teach you; but as the same anointing teaches you concerning all things, and is true, and is not a lie, and just as it has taught you, you will abide in Him.
NKJV

The anointing choses you, you don't chose it Heb 2:4
4 God also bearing witness both with signs and wonders, with various miracles, and gifts of the Holy Spirit, according to His own will?
NKJV
As a result of which the anointing choses your path for you, for example paul was anointed to go and preach the gospel to the gentiles so any time he got to spend time with the jews there was problem. Every anointing finds expression in where it wants you to be, the anointing also controls our actions so that we can effectively be able to do what is given to you for. The spirit of the prophet is subject to the prophet if you are able to control the anointing it will be a great force at use, there are angels assigned to every anointing and if you understand the anointing well then the angels will be able to work effectively with you. When the anointing is given, it takes you into a process of seasons to help you to grow into a place of maturity in its use and still continue growing in the anointing because gradually more is added and new dimensions of the anointing is reveled from stage to stage. In the process of seasons of discovery, you may go through afflictions or challenges and obstacles that the anointing will bring into your path. Ps 66:10-12
10 For You, O God, have tested us;
You have refined us as silver is refined.
11 You brought us into the net;
You laid affliction on our backs.
12 You have caused men to ride over our heads;
We went through fire and through water;
But You brought us out to rich fulfillment.
NKJV
The anointing takes you through it so that you can be good at its use and understand what you have. Sometimes the seasons are repeated, especially if you failed the testing or if a new kind of anointing is given to you. The challenges we may face will be different, but there are seven general patterns, that I have noticed happens to everybody.

The revelation

Every anointing starts with a revelation, when you notice that you have an anointing it could be in the form of visions or dreams like Joseph Gen 37:5-9

5 Now Joseph had a dream, and he told it to his brothers; and they hated him even more. 6 So he said to them, "Please hear this dream which I have dreamed: 7 There we were, binding sheaves in the field. Then behold, my sheaf arose and also stood upright; and indeed your sheaves stood all around and bowed down to my sheaf."

8 And his brothers said to him, "Shall you indeed reign over us? Or shall you indeed have dominion over us?" So they hated him even more for his dreams and for his words.

9 Then he dreamed still another dream and told it to his brothers, and said, "Look, I have dreamed another dream. And this time, the sun, the moon, and the eleven stars bowed down to me."
NKJV, or by direct prophesy, like David 1 Sam 16:12-13
12 So he sent and brought him in. Now he was ruddy, with bright eyes, and good-looking. And the LORD said, "Arise, anoint him; for this is the one!" 13 Then Samuel took the horn of oil and anointed him in the midst of his brothers; and the Spirit of the LORD came upon David from that day forward. So Samuel arose and went to Ramah.
NKJV, saul 1 Sam 10:1

Then Samuel took a flask of oil and poured it on his head, and kissed him and said: "Is it not because the LORD has anointed you commander over His inheritance?
NKJVor Gideon whose was by an angel Judg 6:11-14

Now the Angel of the LORD came and sat under the terebinth tree which was in Ophrah, which belonged to Joash the Abiezrite, while his son Gideon threshed wheat in the winepress, in order to hide it from the Midianites. 12 And the Angel of the LORD appeared to him, and said to him, "The LORD is with you, you mighty man of valor!"

13 Gideon said to Him, "O my lord, if the LORD is with us, why then has all this happened to us? And where are all His miracles which our fathers

told us about, saying, 'Did not the LORD bring us up from Egypt?' But now the LORD has forsaken us and delivered us into the hands of the Midianites."

14 Then the LORD turned to him and said,"Go in this might of yours, and you shall save Israel from the hand of the Midianites. Have I not sent you?"

NKJVand another case was Samson whose parents were told by an angel also. Judg 13:2-5

2 Now there was a certain man from Zorah, of the family of the Danites, whose name was Manoah; and his wife was barren and had no children. 3 And the Angel of the LORD appeared to the woman and said to her, "Indeed now, you are barren and have borne no children, but you shall conceive and bear a son. 4 Now therefore, please be careful not to drink wine or similar drink, and not to eat anything unclean. 5 For behold, you shall conceive and bear a son. And no razor shall come upon his head, for the child shall be a Nazirite to God from the womb; and he shall begin to deliver Israel out of the hand of the Philistines."

NKJV..,.... Judg 13:22-24

22 And Manoah said to his wife,"We shall surely die, because we have seen God!"

23 But his wife said to him, "If the LORD had desired to kill us, He would not have accepted a burnt offering and a grain offering from our hands, nor would He have shown us all these things, nor would He have told us such things as these at this time."

24 So the woman bore a son and called his name Samson ; and the child grew, and the LORD blessed him.

NKJV

Finally, the next way you get revelation is by discovery. You will notice that you are able to do things that are not common to men for instance, you will notice every time you pray for sick persons they are getting healed then you begin to notice that you have a healing anointing. It can be so for different kinds of anointing be it miracles, prophesy, teaching, counseling, and other kinds of anointing.

The battle of the anointing

This is the second stage of the anointing where it starts to fight with you for acceptance and recognition. Any time the anointing comes to someone it will mean many changes to the person's life, and that is very difficult for us sometimes. You will have to make sacrifices and give up things you love and lifestyles you enjoy which can be painful, for many people the cost is just too much to bear. In this stage of the season of the anointing you get into mind struggles because your mind has to be tuned to flow with the anointing you have received, the anointing has a way it wants you to think; apostles think differently from a pastor, the evangelist is also different in his way of thinking from a prophet. Each anointing has you thinking in a way that will enable it to flow, for this reason any time a person becomes anointed you notice that he changes in his nature and thinking but it takes a process which is a battle1 Sam 10:5-7

6 Then the Spirit of the LORD will come upon you, and you will prophesy with them and be turned into another man . 7 And let it be, when these signs come to you, that you do as the occasion demands; for God is with you.

NKJV

When you come to the level of acceptance of the anointing then you will be challenged to know what you have received. Each anointing comes to fulfill a greater purpose than yours, it is a gift,a tool to make way for that purpose to happen. Prov 18:16

16 A man's gift makes room for him,
And brings him before great men.

NKJV

Rom 12:6-8

6 Having then gifts differing according to the grace that is given to us, let us use them: if prophecy, let us prophesy in proportion to our faith; 7 or ministry, let us use it in our ministering; he who teaches, in teaching; 8 he who exhorts, in exhortation; he who gives, with liberality; he who leads, with diligence; he who shows mercy, with cheerfulness.

NKJV

The baptism of fire

After you have accepted the anointing, it baptizes you with power and fire. It empowers you to do things you have never done before. You will notice difference in your life that you are really anointed, and the hand of God is upon you. When jesus new it was time to accept who he was, he went to john the Baptist to be baptized and the spirit came on him and empowered him Matt 3:16-17

16 When He had been baptized, Jesus came up immediately from the water; and behold, the heavens were opened to Him, and He saw the Spirit of God descending like a dove and alighting upon Him. 17 And suddenly a voice came from heaven, saying,"This is My beloved Son, in whom I am well pleased."
NKJV
After king saul accepted the anointing the anointing empowered him to lead Israel to war and break the domination of the philistines 1 Sam 11:6-7
6 Then the Spirit of God came upon Saul when he heard this news, and his anger was greatly aroused. 7 So he took a yoke of oxen and cut them in pieces, and sent them throughout all the territory of Israel by the hands of messengers, saying,"Whoever does not go out with Saul and Samuel to battle, so it shall be done to his oxen."

And the fear of the LORD fell on the people, and they came out with one consent.
NKJV
I have noticed that once you accept the anointing it gives you the authority to control the situations that were at first difficult for you. The reason most people are anointied and not seeing any change in their life is they do not have a deep understanding into what they have been given and so have not fully accepted who they are and what they have. You will notice that for every man or woman of God who is successful they came to a point of revelation when they understood God for themselves and what they are to do for the first time in years before they started to see a turnaround in their lives. Does it mean that the anointing was not there at first? No but they did not understand fully what they had and what was expected of them. Dear reader I want you to understand that you will not do much in the kingdom of God and with your life as a child of God until you get your own personal revelation of God and a deep understanding in your spirit and mind of your destiny and what he expects of you.

The wilderness experience
After you are empowered, you will be confronted with problems and obstacles that will stand in your way to prevent your march to destiny. There is a reason why you are pushed into the wilderness, which is to prove

whether you can handle the level of anointing you have been given, after the first direct healing by peter the church was challenged their answer was to push ahead. That is what we all must do Acts 4:18-21

18 So they called them and commanded them not to speak at all nor teach in the name of Jesus. 19 But Peter and John answered and said to them,"Whether it is right in the sight of God to listen to you more than to God, you judge. 20 For we cannot but speak the things which we have seen and heard." 21 So when they had further threatened them, they let them go, finding no way of punishing them, because of the people, since they all glorified God for what had been done.
NKJV
In the wilderness experience God uses that time to purge you r nature of what he does not like be it your sinful nature, or human nature that will hinder the anointing, and he uses the opportunity to build the divine nature into you. It s a season of trials to bring the best out of you by the way you confront the challenges and obstacles.

The valley of decision
That is the low point of your life at the same time the time that big things can start happening. It is the point you chose to stop or to go forward and change things, it a prat of your life that every discision or choice you make either brings you closer to the anointing or farther away from the anointing. Ithappend in the life of david 1 Sam 30:1-6
1 And it came to pass, when David and his men were come to Ziklag on the third day, that the Amalekites had invaded the south, and Ziklag, and smitten Ziklag, and burned it with fire;

2 And had taken the women captives, that were therein: they slew not any, either great or small, but carried them away, and went on their way.

3 So David and his men came to the city, and, behold, it was burned with fire; and their wives, and their sons, and their daughters, were taken captives.

4 Then David and the people that were with him lifted up their voice and wept, until they had no more power to weep.

5 And David's two wives were taken captives, Ahinoam the Jezreelitess, and Abigail the wife of Nabal the Carmelite.

6 And David was greatly distressed; for the people spake of stoning him, because the soul of all the people was grieved, every man for his sons and for his daughters: but David encouraged himself in the LORD his God. KJV
1 Sam 30:17-19

17 And David smote them from the twilight even unto the evening of the next day: and there escaped not a man of them, save four hundred young men, which rode upon camels, and fled.

18 And David recovered all that the Amalekites had carried away: and David rescued his two wives.

19 And there was nothing lacking to them, neither small nor great, neither sons nor daughters, neither spoil, nor any thing that they had taken to them: David recovered all.
KJV
If david had not encouraged himself and gone after the amelekites he would have lost everything and even his life because the people even wanted to stone him to death as a result of the grief they were in. the moments like this kind is when you discover yourself and form your own personality and identity. But interestingly that was also the turning point of david's life the beginning of his journey to be a great king he was anointed to be. Just after he had survived that problem that he was told that the throne he was waiting for was now available for him to occupy2 Sam 2:1-4

It happened after this that David inquired of the LORD, saying, "Shall I go up to any of the cities of Judah?"

And the LORD said to him, "Go up."

David said, "Where shall I go up?"

And He said, "To Hebron."

2 So David went up there, and his two wives also, Ahinoam the Jezreelitess, and Abigail the widow of Nabal the Carmelite. 3 And David brought up the men who were with him, every man with his household. So they dwelt in the cities of Hebron.

4 Then the men of Judah came, and there they anointed David king over the house of Judah. And they told David, saying,"The men of Jabesh Gilead were the ones who buried Saul."
NKJV
So don't give up on your dream it will be birthed no matter how hot the challenges will be.

The walls of Jericho
That is the stage where the wilderness is over and you must now step out, and take your destiny into your hands and be what you are created to be. It is the place that you break the shackles of the enemy and challenges. It is the stage you stop being defeated, and you start winning.

The release of the anointing
This is the final season that happens, at this state you are mature in the handling of the anointing. You have also proved you self worth and developed confidence in yourself to handle the anointing, as a result of which the anointing is released fully to you for use for what has been entrusted to you and whatever you deem necessary to accomplish your goals in life as far as God is concerned. In as much as the anointing is given to benefits mankind, I have also realized and the Lord has thaught me that the anointing is also for you to use for yourself1 Cor 12:4-8

4 There are diversities of gifts, but the same Spirit. 5 There are differences of ministries, but the same Lord. 6 And there are diversities of activities, but it is the same God who works all in all. 7 But the manifestation of the Spirit is given to each one for the profit of all:
NKJV
Every anointing is for the benefit of all people, which means all including you. Just as the anointing works for people who have faith in it that is the same way it will minister to you if you believe it can work on you. One of the statements Jesus used to make anytime he healed someone or did a miracle was Matt 9:29
"According to your faith let it be to you."
NKJV
If you have faith that the anointing will work for you as it works on others it will. I never knew that until one day, I was waiting on the lord over a personal issue and he explained it to me. He made me understand that what he has given me can also have personal use, I used it for my heart problems, and it just stopped. Since then I have used my anointing on myself if am sick and for my personal problems. Jesus commanded us to

go and preach the gospel and made it clear that in his name, we will cast out devils and we will heal the sick. He did not differentiate the devils that afflict the people of God and the servants of God, all devils are devils so cast that devil in your life out just as you will for a person who comes to you for help. It is the same for sickness he did not differentiate the sick person that it must not be the anointed person but it was every sick person so use your anointing to heal your body when you are sick. Every gift of God is a blessing and not a curse so how can you be a blessing to someone and not be blessed. You are blessed to be a blessing, if you are not blessed you cannot be a blessing to others Gen 12:2

....I will bless you

And make your name great;

And you shall be a blessing.

NKJV

The only thing needed to bring to promises of God to pass in our lives is faith and perseverance

You must also enjoy the benefits of the anointing in you life1 Tim 5:18-19

18 For the Scripture says, "You shall not muzzle an ox while it treads out the grain," and,"The laborer is worthy of his wages."

NKJV

Shield

The anointing is shield for you it protect you from a lot of attacks that would have gotten you Isa 54:17

17 No weapon formed against you shall prosper,

And every tongue which rises against you in judgment

You shall condemn.

This is the heritage of the servants of the LORD,

And their righteousness is from Me,"

Says the LORD.

NKJV

So long as you are anointed and you are serving the Lord, you are protected from every kind of attack unless you are not prudent and careful, but if you rely upon God for protection the anointing will protect you from attacks both spiritual and physical if you will only believe and allow it to work Mark 9:23

23 Jesus said to him, "If you can believe , all things are possible to him who believes."

NKJV
Favor
The anointing brings favor to the anointed personSong 1:3
3 Because of the fragrance of your good ointments,
Your name is ointment poured forth;
Therefore the virgins love you.
NKJV
Ointiment is also oil in the bible so the fragrance of the anointing gives favour to the bearer.
Joy and gladness
The anointing makes you happy Ps 45:7-8
7 You love righteousness and hate wickedness;
Therefore God, Your God, has anointed You
With the oil of gladness more than Your companions.
8 All Your garments are scented with myrrh and aloes and cassia,
Out of the ivory palaces, by which they have made You glad.
NKJV
Health
The anointing makes you healthy if you allow it and don't live a bad lifestyleDeut 34:5-7

5 So Moses the servant of the LORD died there in the land of Moab, according to the word of the LORD. 6 And He buried him in a valley in the land of Moab, opposite Beth Peor; but no one knows his grave to this day. 7 Moses was one hundred and twenty years old when he died. His eyes were not dim nor his natural vigor diminished.
NKJV wh at made moses so healthy because he was enjoying the proviledges of the anointing just as the Israelites since we read thatPs 105:37

37 He also brought them out with silver and gold,
And there was none feeble among His tribes.
NKJV
But prior to that God had told the people were just to obey him and he would heal the so moses acted upon that promise in the anointingGen 1:1 - Ex 15:26
26 and said,"If you diligently heed the voice of the LORD your God and do what is right in His sight, give ear to His commandments and keep all

His statutes, I will put none of the diseases on you which I have brought on the Egyptians. For I am the LORD who heals you."
NKJV
Honor and promotion
The anointing promots you and honors you1 Tim 5:17-18

Let the elders who rule well be counted worthy of double honor, especially those who labor in the word and doctrine.
NKJVJob 29:6-11
6 When my steps were bathed with cream,
And the rock poured out rivers of oil for me!

7 "When I went out to the gate by the city,
When I took my seat in the open square,
8 The young men saw me and hid,
And the aged arose and stood;
9 The princes refrained from talking,
And put their hand on their mouth;
10 The voice of nobles was hushed,
And their tongue stuck to the roof of their mouth.
11 When the ear heard, then it blessed me,
And when the eye saw, then it approved me;
NKJV
If you allow the anointing to work thorugh you it will bring you honor but if you limit it you will not get much out of the anointing and think it is a curse

The secrets of God
The anointing takes you into the presence of God and constant access to God since you are a servant of your master and of the household of God and not a visitor or a guest. Amos 3:7

7 Surely the Lord GOD does nothing,
Unless He reveals His secret to His servants the prophets.
NKJV
The anointing gives you real time access into the plans and purposes of God and the wisdom to use it and to enable his servants to move according to his times and purposes. While at the same time, he gives them his secrets so that they will be able to use it to advance the work that has been committed to him.

Break limitations

The anointing is given to us to break barriers and destroy darkness Isa 10:27

It shall come to pass in that day

That his burden will be taken away from your shoulder,

And his yoke from your neck,

And the yoke will be destroyed because of the anointing oil.

NKJV

By the anointing, we are able to prevail over our enemies and challenges. We are anointed to meet darkness with light and break limitations. We should be able to call things that are not into being, what is missing must be brought into our lives that is why Elisha under pressure could call an end to famine and prophesy an abundance of food for the next day, that is why moses could go to God and bring manna for the his people to eat.

EPILOUGE

The anointing does not change your life significantly, until you use it and contrary to what most people believe, the anointing is not a guarantee of success and liberation of the owner from afflictions. When David was anointed, he went back to being a shepherd. When Saul was anointed, he went back to his father's house until an issue came up that caused him to get angry. Samson had a powerful anointing but he could not do much with his anointing and died a blind man. Yet David used his anointing and built an empire, the bible is full of lots of anointed men and women, some were able to rise to significance but others were never great. Jonah had a unique anointing, an anointing that can convict a city but he never was interested in using it to change lives in fact he run away from his calling. Elijah started to use his anointing and he discovered that the anointing was not enough to change people so he developed a new system of the sons of the prophets and went around teaching them to become good servants of God. Moses had a spectacular anointing but it took lots of wisdom to control and guide the crowd. The anointing consecrates you and empowers use to serve the lord but it is up to you to use it and build something tangible with it. Some people think that the anointing is for personal benefit it is wrong but you do not muzzle the ox that treads the corn, as Elisha told Gehazi 2 Kings 5:26

26 Then he said to him, "Did not my heart go with you when the man turned back from his chariot to meet you? Is it time to receive money and

to receive clothing, olive groves and vineyards, sheep and oxen, male and female servants?

NKJV

It is important to understand that the anointing must not to be abused because each of us will give account of our stewardship of the anointing.

In writing this book, I have tried to lay a foundation for you journey in the anointing I do hope that you learn much and enjoy your journey in the anointing. The anointing is a powerful tool if you use it well it will be greatly to your advantage and will help you to rise to significance but if you do not use it wisely you will labor and have nothing to show at the end of the day. A lot of anointed people suffered for their anointing, Jeremiah became a weeping prophet because the people never listened to his warnings and prophecies, Micah was imprisoned for prophesying about the death of the king. God richly bless you and grant you the wisdom to do well with it.